Baking Without Bounds

A Guide to Delectable Gluten-Free Treats

Ph.D. SARAH BLIGHTLEY

Table of Content

Baking Without Bounds

Introduction

Baking without gluten once seemed an exercise in culinary masochism destined for hockey pucks where fluffy loaves should rise. Yet modern ingenuity transformed pantry staples into masterpieces proving restrictive diets need not limit delight. This cookbook surveys the bounty now possible for gluten-free baking across breads, desserts, and world cuisines.

Within these pages lie tested recipes and techniques for manifesting magic from alternative flours. While tailoring for dietary constraints, we unlock newfound flavors from ingredients long overlooked. Travel through ginger infused breads or experiments with teff alongside rediscovered classics optimized to nourish those who struggle with wheat. Taste empowerment, not exclusion.

Spanning twenty genre-based chapters, this expansive volume chronicles the innovations advancing gluten-free cuisine. It offers both staple formulations as reference and adventurous new combinations drawing inspiration globally. Substitutions adapt traditions to align ethics and enjoyment.

We begin by charting the history of gluten-free diets alongside primer science on suitable ingredients as foundation. Flours milled from roots, nuts, seeds, and grains contain nutritious diversity once obscured by wheat's meteoric rise. From versatile containers like tapioca and arrowroot to ancient grains teeming with protein and fiber, our options overflow. Blend alchemy unfolds.

Baking Without Bounds

Advancing into baking techniques, the book delves into the delicate balance of binding agents, leaveners, and structure builders allowing doughs to rise and set properly. Playing with the ratios of eggs, gums, starches, and alternative dairy unleashes airy results. Here the science and art fuse.

Middle sections traverse every baked category from comforting cookies and quick breads to brunch-time waffles, seeded bagels, elegant cakes then pies oozing fall harvest flavor. Smooth frostings crowning warm muffins and Dialectsavory crackers beckoning thick soups. Each family of sweets unfolds for re-exploration.

As chapters accrue, so do global influences infusing international flairs by fusing coconut milk, matcha, preserved lemons, alternative milks, and healing spices into doughs. Cross-cultural pollination continues the evolutionary arc transcending perceived limits on enjoyment. We bake to gather, not isolate.

In total 300 recipes cascade across continents along with troubleshooting advice honed over years helping students surmount common pitfalls. Options suit every skill level, schedule, and occasion. Several inclusions even sneak extra nutrition through hidden vegetables, seeds, and smart substitutions to nourish guests with each bite.

The resulting landscapes capture culinary freedom despite assumptions around restrictions. They remind us barriers reside not in ingredients but beliefs. Through caring, creativity, and openness, the table expands. Where flour and findings converge, more becomes possible.

Chapter 1

A Brief History of Gluten-Free Baking

The rise in gluten-free living connects to the idea of eliminating foods seen as potentially harmful from one's diet, a nutritional philosophy that gained footing in the late 20th century. As cultural notions of health and wellness have grown more refined, scrutiny has broadened from simply monitoring calorie counts to considering how specific ingredients impact the body and mind. Gluten, a composite of proteins found in wheat and other grains, emerged under this microscope.

In the 1960s and 1970s, gastroenterologists began to associate gluten with celiac disease, an autoimmune disorder whereby the small intestine cannot correctly process the protein. The identification of non-celiac gluten sensitivity further expanded the group of people who benefit, in varying degrees, from a gluten-free regimen. Whereas celiac disease impacts roughly 1% of the population, non-celiac gluten sensitivity may affect up to 13%. These individuals report improved digestion, clearer thinking, balanced energy levels, and other gains when shunning glutenous foods.

Popular health writers have both reflected on and further fueled the rising skepticism of gluten. As early proponents, GF pioneers Alice Bast and Susanna Shore laid educational groundwork in the 1990s and 2000s. Then came a watershed moment in 2011 when physician William Davis published Wheat Belly, a bestselling book positioning modern wheat itself as a "chronic poison." While Davis' thesis outraged mainstream nutritionists, Wheat Belly captivated everyday readers who connected with its central message: that removing gluten can transform one's health, potentially alleviating everything from joint pain to depression.

When celebrities like tennis star Novak Djokovic, talk show host Elisabeth Hasselbeck, and actress Gwyneth Paltrow discussed their positive experiences eliminating gluten, public intrigue grew more feverish. Their testimonies made GF seem not only sensible but glamorous. Coinciding with this publicity was a boom in diagnoses of gluten-related concerns, particularly non-celiac gluten sensitivity.

Baking Without Bounds

As the overall climate grew friendlier toward GF, stores dedicated to specialty products emerged. These retailers brought items that had mainly lived in health food co-ops, like flours milled from ancient grains, onto Main Street. Their bright signage rendered GF shopping conspicuously stylish. Popular blogs and cookbooks provided recipes perfected for alternative flours. Food companies rushed products to supermarket shelves, brandishing a proliferating array of GF labels.

The 2010s became the decade when GF exploded from an obscure medicinal diet to a full-on lifestyle movement centered around vibrant, happy living. This ascent relied on three key pillars: expanding awareness of gluten sensitivity as a legitimate medical concern impacting daily health, endorsement from famous faces tying GF regimens to vitality, and improved access to specialized ingredients and products, allowing home bakers to recreate beloved carb-heavy comforts without gluten.

An excellent fringe benefit of GF's newfound relevance is that it empowers bakers limited by food intolerances to pursue their passion freely. Adjusting recipes to achieve ideal taste and texture without gluten poses an exciting challenge. Experimentation with alternative grains often imparts nutrient density. The necessity of close inspection of ingredients manifests in cleaner eating. Going GF by choice or out of necessity can feel restrictive, yet the world of delightful GF baking options grows more expansive by the day.

Today, gluten-free baking is a norm, but with what we've got here, I hope you've been able to get a good summary of how far it has come. In the next chapter, we'll be looking at the different alternative flour options for a blissful bake.

Ph.D. Sarah Blightley

Chapter 2

Flour Power: Alternative Grain Options

Gluten-free flours made from grains like rice, sorghum, millet, teff, buckwheat, quinoa, and amaranth each have their unique properties that impact the texture and flavor of baked goods. Mastering these alternative flours takes experimentation to find the correct balances and binders for your recipes. Having a guide to their various characteristics helps bake gluten-free goodies with delicious outcomes.

Rice flour, made from grinding rice into a fine powder, proves to be one of the most popular alternative grain options. Types include white, brown, sweet, and glutinous rice flour, each with slight differences. White rice flour creates binding yet crumbly textures, while brown rice flour provides more nutrition and fiber. Sweet rice flour works well for desserts with its hints of sweetness and soft texture. Glutinous or sticky rice flour makes chewy, stretchy doughs perfect for Asian-inspired treats. Begin by swapping about 25% of the wheat flour for rice flour in recipes before adjusting as needed. Extra binders like xanthan or guar gum often help rice flour mimic gluten's elasticity better.

Flours made from tiny grains like amaranth, quinoa, teff, and millet add protein and fiber compared to traditional flours. Creamy amaranth flour shines in crackers, breads, and muffins for texture and flavor. Similarly, ivory-toned teff flour contains iron and calcium for nutrition in pancakes, cakes, and cookies. Subtle millet flour adds a delicate crunch with a mild corn-like taste, while earthy buckwheat flour works for hearty treats like muffins, breads, and pancakes. Start by replacing 10-25% of the wheat flour in recipes with these flours, adding a dash more moisture or eggs if the batter seems too dry.

For those avoiding corn, sorghum flour makes a reasonable substitute in items like cookies, muffins, and cakes. The light tan flour has a mildly sweet flavor and binds well but may yield dense results without adequate leavening. Try swapping about 30% of the wheat flour for sorghum flour, adjusting moisture to achieve the right consistency. Adding a touch more baking powder or yeast can help lift sorghum baked goods, too.

While teeming with nutrients, bran and germ-rich whole grain flours quicken starch damage and bitterness in baked goods. Refined white flours lack these parts, yielding more structure despite less flavor and nutrition. When using whole grain gluten-free flour, stir batters gently, watch oven temperatures, and bake time lengths to prevent over-baking. Substituting 10-30% of the wheat flour with whole grain gluten-free flour makes a good starting point.

Blending two or more alternative flours creates synergy where the flours balance each other's deficiencies. For example, rice flour's crumbly texture gets offset by using half brown rice and half sorghum flour in a recipe. This allows the sorghum flour's binding properties to create better consistency than rice flour alone may lack. Playing with different ratios of various gluten-free flours gives homemade mixes similar to store-bought blends.

When exploring new grains, begin by using established recipes designed explicitly for that flour. Follow procedures closely at first, taking notes on texture, flavor, moisture, and modifications needed. Vary one ingredient at a time to understand its impact. Once familiar with a new flour's quirks, start substituting portions in everyday recipes. Seek binders like xanthan gum to add elasticity at first. Eventually, experimenting with your gluten-free flour blends for homemade recipes lets you control textures and flavors.

While intimidating, remembering a few essential tips makes baking with alternative grain flour rewarding. First, add moisture - ingredients like eggs, oil, milk, or even water help achieve the right batter consistency that gluten provides. Binders like xanthan gum or guar gum also improve elasticity and rise. Second, use proper leavening through baking soda, baking powder, yeast, vinegar, whip egg whites stiff, or chemical leaveners where appropriate. Third, watch oven temperatures, avoiding over-baking items too quickly before setting. Finally, blend two or more flours rather than relying on just one for the best outcomes.

With an open mind to experimentation, a world of alternative grain flour awaits your gluten-free baking. Expect a few flops while finding the right flour combinations, moisture levels, leavening agents, and binders that delight your taste buds. But the journey of discovering new flavors and textures without gluten can be an adventure. Use guides for substitution percentages, follow recipes at first, take good notes, and don't give up. With perseverance, your kitchen can churn out gluten-free cakes, cookies, breads, and more with alternative grain flour that impress any guest. So, how do you get to bind your ingredients together to achieve the best treats? We move to the next chapter, where we get to learn about the best binding agents for your baking.

Chapter 3

Binding Agents: Eggs, Gums, and More

Baking is all about chemistry. Back when I was still in the process of becoming a beginner, a chief chef with whom I was well familiar used to say, "The baker is the scientist." One of those days, he planned to explain what it meant.

"You need an understanding of basic maths to make the best-baked meals." He said. "Baking involves calculation, and the baker calculates everything that gets into the mix in the form of ratios." Understanding the roles of ingredients allows us to tweak and adjust recipes to craft the perfect gluten-free treat. Binding agents play a critical role by creating structure in the absence of gluten, allowing baked goods to hold together properly. Delicious gluten-free baked goods require the right binder and the right proportions. The most common types are eggs, gums, starches, proteins, fats, dairy, and leaveners.

The Mighty Egg

Eggs are one of the most versatile binders. When whipped, eggs trap air bubbles, giving structure to cakes, cookies, soufflés, and quick breads. The eggs coagulate when heated, setting the shape and texture of the baked goods.

Whole eggs act as an emulsifier with lecithin, binding fats and liquids. Egg yolks, in particular, thicken liquids and custards. Savory custards and quiches rely on eggs for thickness and cohesion.

For those avoiding eggs, egg replacers made from starches, gums, and leaveners imitate some of this functionality. Two tablespoons of cornstarch plus two teaspoons of baking powder make an egg substitute for baked goods. But eggs add flavor, color, and nutritional value that replacers cannot fully match.

The Power of Gums

Gluten-free bakers rely heavily on gums and hydrocolloids like xanthan, guar, and psyllium. These soluble fibers absorb moisture and swell to form stretchy networks that trap rising bubbles in the dough. Adding just 0.5-1% of xanthan gum significantly improves the structure, crumb, and moisture of gluten-free bread. Guar and psyllium also strengthen dough without over-stiffening it.

Flaxseeds and chia seeds make eggless binding agents when whisked with warm water. Through the magic of molecular gastronomy, the mucilaginous polysaccharides transform liquids into bouncy gels. A mere tablespoon of ground chia or flaxseed hydrates into the equivalent of three eggs! The resulting gels bind moisture and add nutrients like omega fatty acids. Vegan bakers rely on these miraculous mucilages instead of eggs.

Harnessing the Power of Starch

Starches contribute to the crispness, tenderness, and mouthfeel of baked goods. Starch molecules swell with liquid to form a gel matrix—an edible glue. This gelatinization helps baked goods set, reduces oil absorption for a moister mouthfeel, and contributes to crust formation through dehydration.

Corn starch makes fried foods crispy thanks to a high gelatinization temperature. Potato starch has large swollen granules that create light textures in cakes and muffins. Tapioca starch provides chewiness with its long, sticky molecules. Pure starches lack flavor or nutrition, so they work best combined with nutritious gluten-free flour.

Adding Structure With Protein

Protein content profoundly affects the texture of gluten-free baked goods. Higher protein creates more structure for rising and reduces gumminess in bread. But too much protein causes toughness, so finding the right balance is key. Egg whites and milk proteins help give structure through coagulation and emulsification.

Non-dairy milks vary wildly in protein content, so pay close attention to the best results. Grains like teff, amaranth, quinoa, and buckwheat boost protein levels to improve rising and moisture. Dried milk powder increases structure while adding a lovely buttery flavor. Consider adding a tablespoon per cup of flour.

Harnessing the Power of Fat

The mouthfeel of buttery richness makes baked goods irresistible and satisfying. Fats tenderize textures, help form flaky layers in pastries, carry flavors, and promote moisture retention. Solid fats like butter provide more structure compared to oils. But oils allow for lighter, fluffier textures and resist turning rancid.

When making substitutions, match solid fats with solid fats and liquid fats with liquid fats. And amounts matter—cutting back too much makes goods dry and dense. For best results, choose high-quality, natural sources of fat like butter, virgin coconut oil, avocado oil, and extra virgin olive oil. Their subtle flavors and nutritional content boost any creation.

This concludes the first portion on binders for gluten-free baking. Up next, we explore sweeteners and flavorings in the chapter "Sugar and Spice: Sweetening and Flavoring." Baking is both an art and a science. Understanding ingredients allows us to adjust recipes perfectly for gluten-free success. When ingredients come together in harmony, the results are out of this world!

Egg Replacements for Vegans and Those with Allergies

When it comes to baking, eggs serve multiple crucial roles, from binding to rising to adding richness of flavor. But for those avoiding eggs due to dietary restrictions or allergies, suitable egg substitutes must be used. With the correct alternatives, even intricate custards, airy soufflés, golden pound cakes, and crispy cookies can be egg-free. Through clever use of starches, emulsifiers, vinegar, and commercial substitutes, eggless baking yields impressive results.

Commercial egg replacers made from potato starch, tapioca flour, leaveners, and gums aim to mimic the binding, leavening, and emulsifying properties of eggs. Popular powdered brands allow convenient substitution of eggs in recipes. Whisking the powder with water forms a thick gel that binds moisture. When combined with baking soda or baking powder, bubbles are trapped, just like in beaten egg whites. These replacers work best in cookies and cakes rather than custards. Pre-made liquid egg replacements perform even better, with added gums for enhanced emulsification. However, these products lack the rich flavors and nutrition of eggs themselves.

Baking Without Bounds

When tackling eggless baking, combinations of ingredients help replace some of the functionality of eggs. For binding moisture and adding fat similar to yolks, bananas or pumpkin puree does the trick. These fruit purees not only secure but also add fiber, vitamins, and sweetness. Silken tofu blends into a smooth emulsion for moisture and binding effects reminiscent of eggs. Flax and chia seeds whipped into gel form substitute for up to three eggs, lending critical power with bonus nutrition.

For lift and leavening akin to whipped egg whites, club soda or seltzer adds air bubbles during mixing. Cream of tartar helps stabilize these bubbles, just like in meringues. And vinegar or lemon juice reacts with baking soda for additional rise. When paired with binding ingredients, these leaveners give lift and structure to eggless baked goods.

In custards and quiches, eggs thicken the filling beautifully. Simmering starchy vegetables like potatoes or cauliflower in non-dairy milk creates a nicely thickened puree. Adding a roux of vegan butter and flour also works for thickness and richness. Silken tofu or commercial egg replacer powder lends body as well. These clever tactics yield luscious vegan custard and quiche to please any crowd.

While the art of eggless baking presents challenges, non-egg ingredients powerfully mimic much functionality. When working in combination, everyday pantry items give surprisingly close texture, binding, and rise for egg-free indulgence. A biscuit made with club soda, oil, and chickpea liquid tastes amazingly similar to its eggy counterpart. And a pumpkin flax muffin bursts with moisture and loft, perfectly mimicking the real thing. With practice and persistence, bakers can craft stunning eggless baked goods for all.

So, my dearest baker who is ready to break boundaries, I can imagine you're ready to have some silky snacks held together with the most natural agents, but do you know that doesn't guarantee it would taste perfect? Let's get to that vital element – the taste! How do you get to achieve that perfect taste? We'll learn about this in the next chapter!

Chapter 4

Sugar and Spice: Sweetening and Flavoring

When I first started gluten-free baking, I didn't give much thought to the sweeteners I used. As long as it was sweet, I figured sugar was sugar. However, once I began developing my recipes, I quickly realized that the type of sugar mattered tremendously. Using a suitable sweetener can make or break your baked goods, impacting texture, moisture, browning, and of course, flavor.

In traditional baking, plain white granulated sugar is most often used. But in the gluten-free world, it helps to get more creative with sweeteners. Alternative sugars like coconut sugar or maple syrup bring distinct flavors. And ingredient mixes like xylitol and erythritol can better help items brown and crisp. As you venture into gluten-free sweets, having some sweetener knowledge under your belt is critical.

Gluten-Free Sweeteners

When it comes to gluten-free flours, new options seem to crop up daily. But thankfully, the world of sweeteners is a little more straightforward. Here's a look at some of the most common gluten-free sugar options, along with when and why you'd use them.

Granulated Sugar

Whether beet or cane, plain white granulated sugar is naturally gluten-free, adds a neutral sweetness, and helps baked goods hold their shape once cooked. The refined grains also dissolve and blend in easily. Granulated sugar is ideal anytime you want straightforward, reliable sweetness without altering flavor. Bake it into cookies, cakes, scones, and more.

For most recipes, organic cane sugar can be swapped 1:1 for traditional granulated sugar. It evaporates quickly when exposed to heat. So, it can cause faster browning and crisping at high temperatures. This makes it a nice match for pie crusts, crumbles, biscuits, and other items you want toasted lightly on the exterior.

Brown Sugar

The taste of brown sugar is comforting, calling to mind cinnamon rolls, oatmeal, and other cozy treats. To make it, molasses is added back into refined white sugar. This gives it a delicate butterscotch flavor and damp texture. The molasses also lowers brown sugar's burn point, so it accelerates browning. This makes it ideal for items you want caramelized, like cookies.

When baking gluten-free, swap brown sugar 1:1 for white sugar. But keep in mind the moisture from the molasses requires a slight flour adjustment. For every 1 cup of brown sugar used, add an extra Tablespoon of gluten-free flour to account for the excess wetness. You can easily make brown sugar at home by mixing 1 cup granulated sugar with 1-2 Tablespoons molasses. Light brown uses less, and dark brown uses more. Store it in an airtight jar or bag.

Coconut Sugar

For those avoiding cane sugar, coconut sugar is a nutrient-rich alternative with a low glycemic index. It comes from the evaporated sap of cut coconut blossoms. The sugar retains minerals from the sap, like iron, zinc, calcium, and potassium. It also takes on slight notes of caramel and toffee from the coconut itself.

Use coconut sugar cup-for-cup to replace white sugar. Just know its flavor comes through stronger. So steer clear if you don't want a hint of coconut. It also tends to clump into bricks, which can make accurate measuring annoying. If you live in a humid environment, store your coconut sugar in the refrigerator to prevent hardening.

Maple Syrup

Whether drizzled over pancakes or used in baking, pure maple syrup delights the senses. Graded by color and harvested at different times during syrup season, the varieties range from light amber to dark amber. The deeper the tone, the more pronounced the maple flavor. Maple also brings moisture and a slightly lower sweetness level than plain sugar.

When substituting maple syrup for white sugar, use ¾ cup syrup for every 1 cup of sugar. Lower the liquid in the recipe by about 3 Tablespoons to account for the maple's inherent wetness. Know that maple-baked goods made with it take on a pleasant, sweet earthiness. It pairs exceptionally nicely with nuts, oats, and fall-inspired spices.

Honey

Like maple syrup, honey offers more nuanced sweetness than essential white sugar. The thick, golden liquid is produced by bees from flower nectar. Regional flower differences lead to unique flavors spanning citrus, wildflower, clover, and more. Along with subtle floral notes, honey also contains enzymes and antioxidants.

As another liquid sugar, honey should be subbed at a ¾ cup per 1 cup granulated sugar ratio. Reduce the recipe liquid by 1-2 Tablespoons accordingly. Add about ½ teaspoon of baking soda for every ½ cup of honey used. This helps items baked with honey rise properly despite honey's acidity. One exception – avoid using honey in recipes leavened only by egg whites. Its water content prevents optimal whipping.

Date Sugar

Produced from dehydrated ground dates, this natural sugar retains all the minerals found in fresh fruit (like potassium, phosphorus, and magnesium). It has an earthy sweetness akin to brown sugar. However, date sugar doesn't dissolve easily. So it's best used in muffins, bars, breads, and other dense items instead of delicate cookies or cakes.

Since date sugar clumps, take care to break up any large pieces when measuring it out. And its dryness means you should reduce other recipe liquids slightly. Aim for ½ to ¾ cup liquid removed per 1 cup date sugar added. Date sugar caramelizes quicker than white sugar. So baked goods crisp up faster externally while still staying moist inside.

Fruit Juice Concentrates

Fruit juice concentrates offer another way to impart natural sweetness with pure fruit flavor. Sold frozen or refrigerated, standard options include apple, pear, grape, and pineapple juice concentrates. Each brings the taste you'd expect, often heightened by reduction.

Sub-fruit concentrates for sugar using an equal volume. Since the concentrates add liquid, reduce the recipe liquids accordingly to compensate. And know that fruit concentrates brown faster than plain sugar when baked. So they're excellent for situations where you want a browned exterior or slight caramelization.

Stevia

Unlike the other sweeteners we've covered so far, stevia comes from an herb – not fruit, sap, or cane. Native to South America, the stevia plant produces intensely sweet leaves up to 300 times sweeter than plain sugar. Extracted into a concentrated liquid or powder, stevia offers sweetness without spiking blood sugar.

Gluten-free baking with stevia can't be substituted directly for sugar. Instead, use an erythritol-stevia blend designed specifically for cooking. Other stevia products often contain fillers unsuitable for baking. The erythritol helps mimic sugar's texture, while the stevia brings pure, calorie-free sweetness. Start by substituting the blend for half the sugar in a recipe. Then, tweak to taste from there.

Sugar Alcohols

Sugar alcohols like erythritol, xylitol, and maltitol are considered "artificial" sweeteners. But they're derived from natural sources like fruits, vegetables, and grains. Their molecular structure prevents complete digestion, reducing caloric impact. Sugar alcohols also don't cause sharp blood sugar spikes.

Baking Without Bounds

In gluten-free recipes, sugar alcohol blends can be substituted evenly for ordinary sugar. Benefits include better moisture retention, increased browning and crispness, and avoidance of volume deflation post-bake. If baking with straight erythritol, use about 1 ¼ cup per every 1 cup sugar and increase liquids slightly to compensate for erythritol's moisture absorption.

Reading Labels

With so many natural sweeteners to pick from, reading ingredient labels is vital before using them in gluten-free recipes. Terms like sugar, xylose, and dextrose don't automatically indicate the item is gluten-free. Sugar-whitener wheat starch could be present. Shared equipment might increase cross-contamination risk.

Your best indication is clear "gluten-free" labeling on the packaging. Also, look for certifications from respected allergen control programs like GFP and GMP. When doubts exist, digging deeper on the manufacturer's website may provide more information. Don't be afraid to pick up the phone and call the company if questions remain. For sensitive celiacs, extra care is essential.

While label reading may sound mundane, I've found it dramatically eases the guesswork of gluten-free home baking. Once you've researched brands and identified trusted manufacturers, assembling your pantry becomes much smoother, almost like putting together a baking dream team roster. Except in this case, players like coconut sugar, xylitol, and maple syrup cut!

With your roster rounded out, let's explore how to bake effectively with these gluten-free all-star sugars.

Sweetening Strategies

Granulated white sugar may rank as the standard baking sweetener for good reason. But in gluten-free recipes, branching out brings rewards. Alternative sugars lend moisture, caramelization, and more to transform texture and taste. Savvy gluten-free bakers join multiple sweeteners together, using each to its strengths.

Maybe you combine neutral organic cane sugar for even sweetness with date sugar for flecks of earthy richness—or partner maple syrup's rounded mellowness with stevia's zero-calorie intensity. Coconut sugar could bring a subtle toffee flavor next to xylitol for an awesomely crispy cookie top. The options are wide open.

Thoughtfully blending two or more sweeteners creates depth and nuance. But as tempting as it sounds to throw lots together, restraint wins. Limit sweetener combos to two or three at most. This prevents any one flavor from dominating or reactions occurring. Get acquainted with how each stands alone through single sweetener testing. Once you know their solo personalities, jamming them together becomes the fun part!

Think of building sweetener flavor combos like musical duos. Sometimes, chocolatey brown sugar and deep molasses pair up beautifully, clearing the stage: other times, bright honey and neutral sugar contrast like high soprano with mellow bass. Maple and coconut could be your rock rhythm section. Just be sure to balance the elements. Sudden solo sugar riffs easily overwhelm.

Along with flavor, factor in functional properties too when engineering sweetener teams. For instance, xylitol necessitates a liquid bump, while honey demands extra leavening. Coconut sugar absorbs more moisture than white sugar. Address these nuances so no sweetener feels unexpectedly ignored. Blend based on ratios if needed to keep everything even. Your cookie jars and cake stands will thank you.

Once your sweeteners shine in harmony, it's showtime. Now, let's get baking!

Gluten-Free Sugar Technique

Understanding sweetener characteristics aids recipe development success. But you still need proper sugar technique once the baking begins.

When creaming butter and sugar, for example, incorporated air sets the stage for lift. Cut chilled butter into small cubes first for faster blending. Granulated sugar works best here as alternative sugars may grind less finely. Cream butter alone before adding any sweetener. First, use low speed to loosen and then on high speed to aerate.

Watch for the color change signaling air pockets getting created. Butter transitions from waxy yellow to creamy beige once fluffed up. Now add the sugar a few tablespoons at a time with the mixer running. Scrape down the bowl so the butter fully grabs all granules. Expect the mixture to lighten even further.

Continue creaming until the texture feels grainy yet fluffy. The sugar crystals shear against the soft butter to maximize air bubbles. Too much creaming deflates things. Under-creaming leaves pockets of separated butter and sugar. Getting it just right takes a delicate yet confident hand plus a watchful eye.

When sugar and liquids mix instead, dissolution stands critical. Syrups like maple and honey transition smoothly into batters and doughs. Granulated sugars require heat assistance to dissolve in liquids. Otherwise, lingering sugar crystals and pockets may mar the texture. The more irregularly sized the sweetener, the longer proper dissolution takes.

Getting bakers to dissolve their sugar adequately is a lesson hard learned. Many run liquids and sugars together too quickly, leaving gritty bits behind. Yet nearly burnt caramel isn't ideal, either. Find a middle way – gently stirring over low simmer just until bubbles start and the mass unifies. Soft, blurry edges signal success. Remember – sugar dissolves slowly but burns quickly. Find the sweet spot between not enough warmth and too much intensity. Let your senses guide you.

Caramelization offers another variable to balance when baking gluten-free with sugar. Alternative sugars brown faster thanks to lower smoke points. Useful when desiring browned cookie edges or golden bakery tops, left unchecked, things blacken quickly. Keep peak temperatures in check. Allow time for carryover cooking to finish without charring exteriors to a crisp.

Here, ingredient additions assist. A touch of baking soda lowers sugar's burn threshold for more even caramelizing. Butter also buffers thanks to its fat and evening temperature progression. Liquids like milk or eggs work, too, but steam ventilation from their water content needs consideration. The trick with gluten-free sugar caramelization lies in control. Direct the show firmly yet calmly.

Speaking of steam, sugar also influences gluten-free results through its pull on batter moisture. Granulated sugars absorb ambient liquid as batters rest, while syrups and honey contribute their fluids instead. Accounting for these shifts lets your recipe rise reliably the same way every time. Too dry risks dense results, while overly wet yields gummy textures. Modify liquids given inherent sweetener moisture levels. Allow resting time for absorption equilibrium before the pans go into the oven.

What about post-bake situations like dusting powdered sugar over cupcakes? Here, the lack of gluten causes mainstream powdered sugar-containing corn starch to slide straight off gluten-free crumbs. But powdered sugar made from tapioca absorbs wonderfully. Scan labels to identify gluten-free brands using tapioca instead of corn. Your frosted cakes will thank you for it later through artfully glistening under smooth fondant.

As evidenced throughout, sweets bring some of the most nuanced techniques in gluten-free baking. Master these methods through deliberate attention and patient adjustment. Taste and assess as you go. There's an intuition underlying sugar skill, just as in great musicianship. Let loose and allow your senses to guide you. Move beyond rigid rules into a natural rhythm.

The zen chefs call it "tasting with the whole body." This wider consciousness lets you effortlessly calibrate as needed in real time. Maybe the maple calls for a touch more salt to accentuate flavor. Or the desserts crave a hint of lemon zest to curtail excessive sweetness on the palate over time. Lean into your nonverbal reactions as you sample throughout the bake. The recipe becomes a conversation instead of a unilateral decree. Open up to the call-and-response flowing between you and the sugar.

Then enjoy the symphony unfolding!

High Notes: Sugar Troubleshooting
Even with ample sweetener smarts, gluten-free sugar trouble eventually arises for all bakers. Common issues range from crystallization woes to moisture imbalance mishaps. Monster sweet spots can also attack unexpectedly. Thankfully, most snags are fixed fairly easily. Here are tips for resolving the top sugar snags:

Crystallization
Granulated sugars left sitting may grab ambient humidity and solidify into pesky grains. Caster and berry sugar especially fall prey due to more delicate grains. Avoid crystals by storing opened sugar bags/containers sealed airtight. Adding a pinch of anti-caking cream of tartar discourages clumping, too. If crystals still strike, grind sugar batches into a superfine texture using a food processor or blender again.

2. Moisture Quandaries

Whether too wet or too dry, straying from the sugar's Goldilocks zone spells disaster texture-wise. If things emerge from the oven gummy and gooey, next round cut recipe liquids to adjust for the sugar's hidden hydration pull. Excess liquids draining out of the baked item points toward needing more moisture adjustment. Reverse tactics for crumbliness, adding in touch more wet ingredients to counteract aggressive sugar moisture loss. Reach proper moisture balance through gradual tweaks across successive test bakes to nail consistency.

3. Burning Tendencies

Dark speckling, blackened sections, and acrid flavors all scream sugar-scorching issues. If your gluten-free sweets transform beautifully yet carry bitter charnt undertones, adjustments await. Possible fixes include increasing baking soda, adding butter or milk powders, lowering the oven temp slightly, and tenting/covering items when needed towards the end to prevent excessive top-side caramelization that burns. Watch your bakes extra closely near finish time and modify handling techniques to avoid burn spots.

4. Insufficient Sweetness

Maybe you seek to cut calories by trimming sugar content. Or a new gluten-free flour blend alters absorption properties, diminishing sweet perception unexpectedly. Regardless, gluten-free items flatly lacking in sweetness require attention. First, determine what amount of sugar the recipe truly needs. From there, offset using zero-calorie stevia or erythritol to hit the mandatory level of sweetness without adding unnecessary calories. Taste as you go until the right prominence sings.

5. Sugar Sticking Issues

Exteriors that feel sandy and gritty, even post-bake, signal crystalized sugar needing to be addressed. Humidity likely feeds the excess granulation, especially in drier winter months. Tackle through small liquid increments when mixing – don't dump all liquids in at once. Cover dough rounds in between kneading if they feel especially gritty. As mentioned before, cream of tartar helps impede crystal growth, too. Adjust handling and storage to curb sticky sugar syndrome!

Gluten-Free Baking: The Sweet Life

While I hoped to cover choosing sweeteners extensively here, entire books could be written on gluten-free sugar alone! Its complexity continues, intriguing bakers and dessert lovers ceaselessly. Perhaps that allure comes from sugar's Grund element – delight.

We don't indulge in gluten-free chocolate chip cookies because they offer balanced nutrition. No one craves pumpkin pie for its vitamin richness. Sugar fills a soul space beyond nutrients and sustenance. It feeds our craving for joy. Each birthday cake, frothy milkshake, and candy heart points toward sweetness itself

Pumpkin Pie Spice
The blended warmth of cinnamon, ginger, nutmeg, and allspice brings guaranteed coziness. Lean into full tilt for autumnal pies and breads. But a sprinkle also brightens up sugar cookies and cupcakes year round. For those sensitive to cinnamon, try swapping it for maple sugar in the blend instead.

Garam Masala

This foundational Indian mixture combines up to 12 spices ranging from black pepper to mace. Added early, the heat amplifies, while late addition toward the end blooms its aroma. Partner garam masala with sugars like coconut and jaggery in gluten-free chai cakes. Or add intrigue to fruit crumbles and crisps.

Chinese Five Spice
Fusing licorice-like anise with peppery Sichuan peppercorns, this blend brings a captivating balance. The mix accents gluten-free pork dishes magically but also crossover into sweets astoundingly well. Its gentle spiciness pairs famously with gingerbread, honey, and molasses. Infuse your sugar cookies or quick bread batters for a multi-dimensional taste.

Middle Eastern Baharat
Arabic for "spice", this heady combo contains up to 14 ingredients like rosebuds and coriander. The complexity shines and is spotlighted next to yogurt, sesame, and pistachios in frozen desserts or creamy cheese-based sweets. Think lush cardamom ice cream with honeyed aharat baklava nestled inside. Or tangy lemon curd tarts topped with toasted Bharat pistachios.

Herbes de Provence
Common in European dishes, this herb mix offers floral notes. Lavender, rosemary, thyme, and fennel pollen mingle brightly with berry sugars and wine reductions. Include herbes de Provence when poaching summer fruits in Shiraz or crafting rhubarb sorbet. The herbs prevent one-note sweetness for sophistication. Kick up honeyed cornbread, too, for brunch.

While endless spice blends tempt, restraint prevents muddiness. Pick a single standout or narrow complimentary combo in any recipe. Familiarize yourself with each flavor independently before blending spices. Pay attention to intensity variances across companies and batches. Personalize preferred strengths over time. Mastering spice layers may take patience, but it unlocks new dimensions of mouthwatering gluten-free potential!

Extracting Flavor
Alongside herbs and spices, extracts elicit taste, too. From fruity essences to floral infusions, bottled extracts make baking magic. Here are my gluten-free go-to's for amplifying sugar.

Vanilla Extract
This baking essential combines alcohol and vanilla bean infusion for quintessential flavor. Pure vanilla with visible specks marks quality. Unfortunately, clear artificial vanilla still abounds on grocery shelves – skip it. The complex sweetness plays well in nearly all gluten-free desserts. But shine it spotlit in cream sauces, custards, ice creams, and French pastries.

Almond Extract
Underutilized in home baking, this punchy extract livens up sugar beautifully. Just a small amount conveys aromatic toasted nuttiness. Partner in moderation with stone fruits, honey, chocolate, and spices like cardamom. Almond extract stars in nut-based gluten-free flours too, like almond meal. Try it elevated in marzipans, frangipanes, and traditional Basque gateaus.

Peppermint Extract

Nothing says festive like peppermint's cooling crispness. This extract, made from mint oil packs serious flavor power. A little goes a long way to energize cookies, candies, ice creams, and more. For year-round convenience, keep peppermint extract on hand instead of fussing with fresh herbs. Mix with dark or white chocolate or combo with winter fruits like cranberry and pomegranate.

Orange Extract

Bright citrus orange extract adds sunshine and vitamin C vibrancy to gluten-free desserts. If you like amplified orange zest without grating mess, this provides a handy shortcut. Made from orange peel oil, quality brands taste freshly squeezed. The extract uplifts pound cakes, donuts, sugar cookies, and quick breads magnificently. Lime extract by the same makers carries similar benefits.

Rose Extract

Regal and decadent, edible rose extract transports gluten-free delicacies to gourmet heights. Intensely perfumed like Turkish delight candy, a drop or two sumptuously scents sugar-based creations. From rosewater panna cottas to rose-infused macaron shells, possibilities mesmerize endlessly. Look for natural rose extract without artificial additives for purity. Then channel your inner Parisian patisserie chef!

Foodie Trends: Sugar With Soul

Beyond usual cake and cookie routes, innovative gluten-free artisans lead the way, fusing global flavors into awe-inspiring sugar expressions. Follow their lead, lifting your gluten-free dessert game through cross-cultural influence.

Gluten-Free Jaggery Custards

Jaggery is concentrated raw cane juice often used in Indian cuisine. With earthy complexity similar to molasses, it combines gorgeously with classic custards. Toast the jaggery lightly to amplify its malted flavor. Then, infuse into gently set egg custards enriched with cardamom and saffron. Serve warm or chilled in individual ramekins as the perfect light-yet-lush cross-cultural dessert.

Sweet Tamale Cakes

In Mexico, gluten-free corn husk tamales enjoy holiday fame. For your own celebration-worthy take, bake tamale-inspired cakes instead! Make tender gluten-free cornbread dough, then add butter, sugars, chocolate chunks, spices, and soaked corn husks. The husks impart festive vegetal notes while maintaining moisture. Finish the unique mini-cakes with cinnamon cocoa whipped cream. ¡Delicioso y diferente!

Brazilian Brigadeiros

Traditionally enjoyed at birthday parties in Brazil, these truffle-like sweets beckon global fame. Condensed milk is combined with butter and chocolate sprinkles and then hand-rolled into bite-sized balls. From there, the possibilities fly. Roll brigadeiros in coconut or nuts for texture. Vary the chocolate type used, like white chocolate with lime zest. Or make brigadeiro ice cream sundaes draped in homemade dulce de leche with candied orange peel.

Gourmet Cookie Cups

Why serve gluten-free cookies flat when you can pipe them into edible vessels instead? Fill piped cookie cups with ice cream, mousses, curds, or hand-whipped cream once baked. Options for global flavors abound. Maybe lemon pistachio cups filled with blood orange avocado cream. Or Mexican chocolate cookie cups topped with dulce de leche and sea salt. Endless delights await your gluten-free cookie jar "barware"!

Vegan Pavlovas

Traditional pavlovas encase fruit and cream in airy meringue shells, paying homage to Russian ballerina Anna Pavlova. For a creative spin, try gluten-free, plant-based versions! Whip aquafaba into glossy peaks as the base, gently folding in sugars, nondairy milk, and vinegar. Then, bake into crisp-shelled vessels for holding coconut yogurt mixed with mango chunks, lychee, and mint. Top with crystallized ginger or lemongrass caramel sauce for added decadence. Graceful, global, and gluten free!

The culinary creative possibilities stretch boundless when you view the world pantry as your playground. Let global flavors inspire your own signature gluten-free spins. With so many cultures and ingredient options at your fingertips these days, spectacular fusions await daily.

I challenge you to pick a lesser known sugar like panela, rapadura, or jaggery. Then, scan cultural desserts featuring that sugar as a focal point. Which native herbs, fruits, nuts, and spices star alongside traditionally? Note the local flair and traditional preparations.

Finally, envision your own updated homage with these dynamic flavors migrated into gluten-free territory. Maybe Ugandan ginger-spiced, rapadura-sweetened fritters filled with garlicky millet mousse and topped with hibiscus tea gelatin or Peruvian purple corn syrup-soaked plantains layered with quinoa ginger cake and lucuma lime curd. Or Mexican chocolate chile cake made with smoky chipotle pane.

Chapter 5

Yeasted Breads: Rises and Shines

Who else is deeply in love with yeasted bread? In contrast to the other major forms of bread, like quick breads, yeast breads are produced using yeast, as the name indicates. When yeast is coupled with sugar and warm water, it multiplies and releases carbon dioxide. This, in turn, produces a soft loaf of bread when combined with dry ingredients. In this chapter, I'll walk you through the process of making the perfect yeast bread that rises and shines.

Making a Basic Gluten-Free Yeast Bread

As intimidating as kneading dough may seem, gluten-free yeast breads are very approachable! With a few guidelines outlining the core ingredients and basic techniques, even novice bakers can achieve light and fluffy loaves right at home.

Our journey begins with an example recipe for a simple sandwich-style white bread. While enriched breads often rely on wheat flour for stretchy gluten strands that trap rising air bubbles, there are great substitutes that perform similarly in gluten-free baking. Rice flour, tapioca starch, potato starch, and xanthan gum make an excellent foundation.

The starches contribute texture, while the gum mimics gluten for structure. With yeast for steady rises, eggs for richness, oil for moisture, and sugar for food, this combination creates all the lift and softness of traditional yeasted bread!

Now, onto the procedure! After mixing the dry and wet ingredients separately, combine them to form a shaggy mass and begin kneading. Don't worry if the dough starts sticky; additions of extra flour while kneading help it take shape. Once the dough becomes smooth and elastic, set it aside to rise, covered and undisturbed. Watch as it slowly doubles in size thanks to the carbon dioxide produced by active yeast! This first rise develops flavor compounds and sets the gluten substitute to withstand the expansion of gases.

After the rise completes, gently punch down the dough to release trapped air before shaping it into a loaf pan. Careful handling prevents overworking at this stage, which can damage the structure. Allow a second shorter rise for added lift. While the shaped dough rises once more, preheat the oven to ensure it reaches optimal baking temperature in time.

Finally, the best moment arrives! Bake the risen loaf until golden on top and hollow-sounding when rapped. The crust browns while moisture transforms into steam, giving rise to that signature domed shape and light crumb inside. Cool completely before slicing to prevent gummy textures. Enjoy this nourishing loaf on its own or use it for sandwiches—no one ever has to know it's gluten-free!

Stops Along the Way: Add-Ins for Texture and Flavor

Now that we've explored the core method for a basic gluten-free yeast bread, let's visit some fun destinations along our bread-baking journey to discover new ingredients to try! These add-ins bring flavors, textures, colors, and added nutrition to our loaves.

We'll start with seeds, an easy addition that packs crunchy bites into every slice. Sunflower, sesame, poppy, flax, and pumpkin are all fair game. Toast them lightly first to intensify their flavor before mixing them throughout the dough during kneading. The rough surfaces grab onto the developing gluten strands, securing the seeds neatly into the crumb. They toast up again to a beautiful golden shade during baking.

Dried fruits also feel right at home in bread, contributing chewy, sweet bursts in every bite. Raisins are a classic choice, as are dried cranberries, cherries, blueberries, mango, papaya, pineapple, and apricots...the options span the produce aisle! For even distribution, chop large fruits into smaller pieces before incorporating them into the dough. To prevent sinking, consider dusting chopped dried fruit with a bit of tapioca or potato starch first.

In the same chewy category, mix-ins like chocolate chips, butterscotch chips, peanut butter chips, toffee bits, chopped nuts, shredded coconut, and cocoa nibs are always crowd-pleasers. Their creamy or crunchy textures intersperse nicely amidst the soft crumb. Melty chocolate chips, in particular, create lovely pockets of gooey richness when the bread is toasted. Just take care not to overmix once these fragile mix-ins are added, or they might disappear into the dough!

For savory bread, ingredients like caramelized onions, roasted garlic, sun-dried tomatoes, olives, cheese, and assorted herbs take center stage. Knead them in gently to retain their textures. Roasted vegetables like potatoes, bell peppers, zucchini, or butternut squash also transition beautifully into dough, having absorbed plenty of flavorful browning during their initial cooking.

And let's not forget cheese for its salty savoriness! Finely grated hard cheeses like parmesan, cheddar, gouda, and asiago infuse dough with delightful punches of umami. Softer crumbled cheeses like feta, goat cheese, and blue cheese make lovely pockets that melt into tangy deliciousness during baking. A herbed cheese bread with sundried tomatoes makes an impressive and colorful statement slice!

For sweet inclinations, cinnamon, cardamom, vanilla bean, citrus zest, ground ginger, cocoa powder, matcha powder, berries, maple syrup, honey, and brown sugar all lend warm, energizing flavors. Kneading releases their aromatic essential oils, allowing maximum infusion into the loaf. With a sprinkle of streusel topping, swirled pumpkin bread, lemon poppyseed loaf, and chocolate babka, make excellent additions to a brunch spread!

When adding any mix-ins, moderation is key to prevent unbalancing the main dough. As delightsome as chocolate chunks or berry compote can be, overdoing it compromises the structure and rise. Get creative exploring combinations, but keep add-ins below a quarter portion of the overall dough weight. And resist peeking under the hood too much during rising and baking as tempting aromas begin to release! Patience pays off in the form of high, handsome loaves.

Of course, the ideas only start here - play, wander, and discover on your own! Every bread journey leads to new horizons, so bake beyond labels. Now, let's shift gears to discuss...

Rising to the Occasion: Alternative Leavening Agents

While active yeast cultures produce the bulk of lift in most gluten-free recipes, other leavening agents contribute lightness too. Used judiciously in combination with yeasted bread, these ingredients provide extra insurance for high rises with bonus flavors to boot!

Cultured buttermilk and yogurt contain live cultures that generate bubbles during fermentation and baking. The tangy flavor of buttermilk suits bakery-style sandwich bread, while yogurt shines alongside nuts, seeds, honey, and fruit. Allow extra time for these cultures to produce gases compared to standard yeast.

Whipped eggs act similarly to stretch and trap air into bread dough. For challah, brioche, and other enriched doughs, separating eggs and whipping the whites individually before gently folding them into the complete batter helps achieve supreme lightness!

In the chemical leavening arena, baking soda and baking powder both produce carbon dioxide bubbles upon mixing with moisture and heat. For quick breads, muffins, and scones leavened without yeast, they kickstart the rise efficiently. Adding a touch to yeasted bread dough gives the yeast a head start generating lift. Acidic ingredients like lemon juice, buttermilk, chocolate or honey must be present for chemical leaveners to activate properly. Too much causes over-rise and collapse.

Last but not least, steam from moisture converts to vapor during baking, expanding to beautifully lift delicate pastries. In croissants, the buttery layers achieve incredible height thanks to the liquid-to-gas transformation. So even without kneading or rising time, moisture fuels lift!

While yeast does most of the yeoman's work, leavening gluten-free doughs, complimentary agents provide additional insurance. Supporting starches, gums, eggs, and leaveners ensure our breads reach inspiring heights worthy of a standing ovation! Now, let's explore more steps along the road...

Shaping Up: Alternative Vessels for Rising and Baking

Thus far on our journey, we've worked mainly with rectangular loaf pans, assuming standard sandwich-style boules, baguettes and loaf shapes. But gluten-free dough also fills a myriad other vessel shapes beautifully! Oval bundt pans, Pullman tins, ring molds, fluted brioche pans and even sphere-shaped bowls guide dough into stunning transformations.

Ramekins and muffin tins provide perfect single-serve options in both sweet and savory versions. Hearty bread bowls hold steaming soups and stews. Braided challah, spiral cinnamon rolls and folded calzones will stop guests in their tracks when revealed!

Traditionally shaped bagels, soft pretzels, and English muffins require poaching or boiling before baking to develop delicious crusts. Sturdy semolina or cornmeal-dusted pizza peels easily launch hand-shaped rounds dotted with creative toppings. Even a simple circle of fat or thin dough bakes up crisp yet chewy in style.

Gluten-free sandwich breads also fill cute mini tin loaf pans for whimsical shapes. Pull-apart monkey bread makes a sweet, nostalgic treat for kids, while mini tea loaves gift-wrapped present beautiful edible offerings. Hollowed braided knot rolls secured with a glaze offer the perfect vessel for soup dunking.

And the play continues with enrobed bread! Thick slices cloaked with melted chocolate or warm caramel sauce elevate French toast, pudding, and ice cream exponentially. Hand pies fold decadent fillings neatly capped in a blanket of bread. Turnovers, hot pockets, calzones, pot pies, pasties, empanadas — with two disks of dough, the flavor combos become endless!

While most any vessel can hold gluten-free dough, the thickness directly affects the baking time and temperature needed. Thinner shapes like pizza or flatbreads cook faster at higher heat, while thicker loaves require more time at moderate temperatures. Inserting an instant-read thermometer helps test for doneness between 190- 210°F. The crumb should appear set without doughy streaks or wetness. Continue baking regular or mini loaves for 5 to 10 minutes more if the interiors seem underdone.

Holiday breads magnify in grandeur, shaped as wreaths dotted with fruits and nuts, braided egg challah, panettone towering with dried fruits, or intricately iced stollen dusted with powdered sugar. Even savory mixes encased in pastry dough for beef wellington or coated with cheese in cordon bleu heighten celebration fare.

While almost any vessel can contain the wonder that is gluten-free dough, creativity in shaping beyond loaves opens new frontiers. Sculpt breads to match occasions or whims by seeing pans as gateways to adventure. Now, onwards, we continue to...

Rising Stars: Sourdough and Enriched Breads

Traveling deeper along our path to artisan breads, let's take a turn towards that revered rise-master sourdough next. Unlike standardized packets of commercial yeast, true sourdough culture features a community of wild yeast strains, lactic acid bacteria, and sometimes dairy ferments selected over time for their vigor and flavors. The sour tang comes from acids breaking down starches into sugars to feed the microbes. And the bubble-producing powerhouse relies not on volume but on activity and stamina!

A well-kept sourdough starter doubles in size 8 to 12 times at room temperature, given regular feedings. And that lifting force translates beautifully into gluten-free breads! The key lies in strong starches, awaiting activation by sourdough's acids. Once incorporated into a dough with a full dose of starter, buckwheat, teff, sorghum, cassava flour, and more, build a gorgeous oven-spring and open crumb worthy of any artisan bakery.

Start with liquid levain builds for increased hydration, fermented overnight in step-downs for full flavor development. Use gentle mixes to finish and minimize deflating the established rise. Patience through long, cool fermentation allows yeast and bacteria full reign to produce gases, transform sugars, and build character and texture. This alchemy relies on time, not commercial booster additives!

The resulting loaves showcase all the hallmarks of coveted sourdough: crackly crusts that shatter into shards when torn, extremely tender stretchy crumbs with irregular holes, pleasant tang that sparks salivation, and unparalleled keeping qualities without preservatives. What's not to love?

Baking Without Bounds

Beyond levain breads, soakers, and Bigas, using sourdough starters or discarded mother liquid from feedings also incorporates wonderful fermented flavor into doughs. Adjust starter percentages to balance acidity, letting time tame its bite. The dormant gluten substitute starches require more finessed coaxing than wheat to awaken, but with wise handling, the results are astounding!

Venturing in the reverse direction, enriched doughs spotlight butter, eggs, and sugar instead of sourness. The fat coats proteins, allowing more spread before the structure sets to create an open crumb yet fine texture. Fats restrict gluten formation, preventing toughness. Enriched brioche and challah thus bake impossibly soft and pillowy despite their deceptive simplicity!

Buttery croissants encapsulate the enriched concept with ethereal, shattery results. Though requiring significant finesse, laminated gluten-free doughs absolutely can rival wheat versions! Using rested dough and cautious rolling improves the extensibility of thin sheets. Chilling each fold firms the dough to prevent oozing and maintain distinct layer separation. Egg washes with whole milk or cream boost pliancy and sheen, guarding against dryness. During baking, ice baths delay shape loss by rapidly chilling as the butter melts. Take care not to underproof during the rises or the delicate structure collapses!

Both sourdough's acidic ferments and enriched dough's fat and sugar aid our quest for impressive lift without wheat's elastic gluten. Master these pillars to rule artisan baking realms proudly with your gluten-free breads! Their impressive keeping qualities ensure enjoyment for days...if they last that long before devouring! Now rising to the apex, we next reach...

Chapter 6

Quick Bread: No Yeast Required

We've got the hang of the process for the baking of the perfect yeast bread. But yeast breads are not all there is to it! Now, we're going to be discussing quick bread. Firstly, what are quick breads? In simple terms, quick bread is a type of bread recipe that doesn't use yeast. That's all there is! Instead of using yeast to make the bread rise, these recipes use leavening agents such as baking soda and baking powder. Quick breads are different from yeasted breads because they don't require proofing or kneading. Let's go over all there is to this type of bread in this brief chapter.

Mixing the Batter

The art of mixing smooth, lump-free, gluten-free quick bread batters relies on a delicate balance of ingredients and technique. As we explore unleavened baking delights from muffins to scones and more, proper mixing paves the path to sweet success.

Our journey commences with dry and wet ingredients measured to perfection. Scooping flours made from rice, sorghum, and tapioca transport us to fields waving gold under summer sunlight. Spices conjure visions of faraway markets filled to bursting with vivid pyramids of cumin, ginger, and cinnamon.

Crystalline sweeteners as white as snow or dark as molasses connect us to both field and factory. And wet ingredients like eggs, milk, and oils elicit pastoral scenes rich with animals and plants. Each component sings its melody, but the ensemble awaits our direction.

Arrange dry elements in one vessel and wet in another to avoid premature blending. Spoons glide through contents, aerating grains so lightly they threaten to take flight. Spatulas traverse mixing bowls, leaving furrows like a farmer's plow. As we gradually add liquid to dry, textures transform from crumbly and cracked to cohesive dough. Sturdy wooden spoons steer batters on the route toward emulsion. We massage out lumps and pockets of ingredients not yet harmonized. With care and patience, contents meld into a unified velvety cream.

With well-combined batters ready for baking, visions of tea cakes, scones, and loaves golden brown emerge. Batters turn to bread in the alchemy of oven warmth, their surface cracks resembling parched earth. Cooling racks offer rest to loaves fresh from the fire. A pat of butter melting into a crumb signals the first delicious bite. Our gluten-free quick breads hold richness as much in taste as memory, binding together seasons, soils, and friendships into one humble loaf.

Now we turn to shape batters with care, as a potter molds soft clay. Scoops dispatch heaps onto pans like drops of rain pooling on a window. Here, the batter transforms once more from loose to solid as living roots reach deep into the soil. Into the oven for alchemy, where gentle heat rouses dough to life. Soon, fragrant, tempting loaves emerge to draw us near.

But restraint and patience are needed lest we scorch untempered palms on hot rounds. Instead, we let cookies, scones, and baked goods rest awhile, observing steam spiraling up through the crackled crust. When air is at last still and cooling transformation concludes, then we taste, at last, sweet labor's fruits.

That brings us to the end of this chapter, aiding us in telling the process involved in quick bread and yeasted bread apart. Enjoy your next bake!

Chapter 7
Cookies: Crispy, Chewy, Classic

From ultrathin and delicate shortbread to chunky, chewy chocolate chip, cookies are a classic treat that never goes out of style. Gluten-free bakers need not miss out on it thanks to an array of flours and techniques for crafting crispy, chewy, melt-in-your-mouth perfection. What's a baker without being able to make the kids smile with some lovely cookie options? Let's go over all the different types of cookies for your next baking.

Mixing and Baking Cookies

For best results, allow all ingredients like butter, eggs, and milk to come to room temperature before mixing. Cold ingredients can inhibit cookies from spreading properly or result in uneven textures. Creaming the butter and sugar together introduces air pockets that expand in the oven for lightly aerated cookies. Meanwhile, cutting in chilled butter using various flours produces shortbread and tart shells with wonderfully flaky textures.

Different mixing methods, like creaming versus just stirring, impact the texture and shape cookies take on during baking. Overmixing causes gluten formation, so for most gluten-free batters, this isn't a concern.

However, overworking starch-heavy batters activates starches that result in unpleasantly tough or gummy cookies. Mixing serves to distribute wet and dry ingredients evenly. Undermixing leads to uneven baking with raw flour taste and hard bits from undissolved starch.

Baking soda and powder are essential raising agents for cookies. Double-acting baking powder works twice, first upon mixing with liquid, then again upon heating. Excess causes too much expansion, leading to craggy, cracked tops. Not enough raising agent and cookies spread out instead of rising up, resulting in dense hockey pucks lacking texture. Other ingredients like beaten eggs or whisked heavy cream add air to cookie batters, helping them rise without harsh chemical leaveners.

Portioning cookie dough uniformly ensures even sizes and consistent baking. The classic ice cream scoop divides dough into reliably round balls that hold shape on baking sheets. For perfectly uniform bars and logs, a scale weighs dough pieces with precision. Individual wrappers for slice-and-bake dough balls eliminate waste from leftovers going stale. Fill cookie scoops to the rim without packing or compressing for ideal rising potential.

Most cookie recipes call for baking from a frozen state or chilled dough to minimize spreading and promote rising. As air pockets created from whisking and creaming expand upon contact with heat, refrigerated dough holds its shape better. Exceptions include slice-and-bake logs, hand-shaped doughs, and icebox pinwheel cookies requiring shaping before chilling to set the form. Allow such doughs about 20 minutes of working time at room temperature to promote pliability when forming intricate shapes.

Baking Without Bounds

Correct parchment paper lining prevents sticking issues when transferring delicate cookies off hot baking sheets. Reusable silicone baking mats withstand high heat for repeated use, though they impart subtle texture to cookie bases. Insulated cooling racks prevent overbaking from residual heat in baking sheets, heating cookies after removal from ovens. Stack racks over dinner plates to catch stray drips of molten chocolate or errant sprinkles of sugar glaze. Leave space between racks when layering for optimum airflow to quicken cooling and set cookies before serving or storing.

Baking times vary with factors like ingredient ratios, cookie thickness, and oven temperatures. Thick hunks require longer stays in dry heat to evaporate moisture, causing sunken middles or unpleasant clamminess. Conversely, thin sugar cookies risk becoming bitter when overbaked. Oven temps between 325-375°F strike a balance to activate rising agents without scorching delicate doughs, though testing remains key for new recipes. Start testing a minute or two before the minimum suggested time and let visual and tactile clues like firm edges and dry tops determine when they are properly baked through.

Cookies continue cooking after removal from ovens due to residual heat from baking sheets and buildup in linings. Letting rest prevents overbaked interiors that crumble apart upon biting or handling. Lighter doughs prone to spreading, like macaroons and meringues, benefit from gradual cooling to set structure without collapsing. Transfer finished cookies onto racks with sufficient spacing to encourage airflow from all sides. Stack rounds in alternating diagonal lines like brickwork rather than flats to allow steaming moisture to dissipate.

Decorating before baking requires planning ahead for toppings set in place rather than melting and sliding into pools on cookie surfaces. Vanilla sugar's finer texture disperses more evenly into doughs for thorough flavor infusion compared to coarsely grated whole pods with clumped seeds. Candied ginger needs chopping into pea-sized bits for even distribution throughout chewy molasses cookies. Rougher sanding or sparkling sugars add a gritty crunch, while delicate dissolvable pearl dustings lend an elegant shimmer. Press decorating sugars and crushed peppermint lightly into dough rounds before baking so pieces anchor into puffed surfaces rather than skittering off onto baking sheets.

Post-baking finishes range from drizzled glazes needing to be set up to sprinklings of powdered sugar best showered over warm surfaces to adhere. Allow about 5 minutes for recently baked cookies to firm up if applying runnier icings like lemon or vanilla that require some penetration into the crumb. Start with thinned consistencies to encourage absorption, then adjust to nape the back of a spoon as the topping starts to pool on cookie surfaces rather than integrate. Reserve any chunky accompaniments like crushed toffee or chopped nuts to sprinkle over finished plain glazed cookies for a textural contrast.

Nutrient-rich mix-ins enhance both flavor and wellness appeal with antioxidants and energizing whole grains. Toasted quinoa flakes, puffed millet, and crispy brown rice cereal lend a hearty crunch in place of gluten-rich oats for granola-inspired cookies with a twist. Sunflower and pumpkin seeds pack roasty warmth, while dried fruits like apricots and cherries contribute chewy bites without excess sugars. Chop or grind chunks into smaller pieces for even inclusion throughout cookie batters rather than unwieldy whole slices crowding each bite. Blend such textural contrasts with classic flavors like ginger, molasses, vanilla, and cinnamon.

Baking Without Bounds

Replacing some all-purpose alternative flour called for in cookie recipes with almond or coconut varieties lends richness and tender crumb. Start by subbing in 15-25% of the total flour amount with similarly finely milled nut meals or shreds to avoid gritty textures. Too much coconut flour absorbs extra moisture, resulting in dry and crumbly cookies. Almond flour imparts more pronounced nutty notes though less sweetness than wheat flour. Balance its mildly bitter edge by upping sugar quantities by a tablespoon or two as needed for preferred levels of sweetness.

Despite the name, slice-and-bake doughs often benefit from at least 15-30 minutes of chilling after slicing to help seal cookie edges and prevent spreading upon baking. Start by slicing logs into evenly sized rounds no thicker than ¼ to ½ inch maximum for ideal interior to exterior cookie ratios in the finished treats. Chilling allows dough surfaces reexposed to air to firm up for better structural integrity, staying neatly composed on baking sheets. Take care when transferring sliced dough rounds to prevent mashing delicate shapes, and decorate with sanding sugars or citrus zest before freezing completely for long-term storage.

Hand-shaped cookies allow for custom contours like fluted edges, central divots perfect for dolloping jam fills, and inventive cutouts showcasing seasonal motifs. Freeze details like pastry tips, tiny cookie cutters, or embossed rolling pins before pressing them into pliable doughs to set intricate designs without handling melting and softening during shaping. Work swiftly or chill dough repeatedly as needed between batches to maintain crisp impressions that hold shape upon baking rather than losing definition.

Icebox pinwheel cookies delight with their kaleidoscopic swirls of contrasting batters swirled together. The defining characteristic comes from blending two separate doughs – typically one flavored vanilla and the other chocolate or spice for visual contrast. Each gets an initial chill to form workable disks before stacking and rolling together into logs that then get sliced to reveal signature striations. Cookies puff into matte and shiny layers, revealing cinnamon bursts or fudgy ripples in the cross-section.

Baking Cookies: Key Troubleshooting Tips

Cracking or spreading out cookies points to too much rising agent or leavener in the recipe. Amp up the structure to contain bubbles with an extra egg white or a tablespoon of ground flax seeds whisked into the batter. Or decrease baking soda and powder amounts by about 20% in future attempts for less volatility from trapped air expanding. Rotating sheets midway through baking also helps prevent lopsided spreading toward back heated oven walls.

Pale doughy centers that resist baking through indicate cookie slices are too thick or batches overcrowded on sheets, limiting airflow. Use an ice cream scoop with a release lever to portion uniform balls of dough rather than uneven hand shaping. Increase spacing to at least an inch apart on all sides and bake in batches to allow proper air circulation for direct heat contact all around.

Chalky cookie texture with a coarse mouthfeel relates to undissolved lumps of starch granules or crystallized sugar. Make sure to cream butter and sugar thoroughly until fluffy and pale in color. Or use liquid sweeteners like agave, maple syrup, or honey that emulsify more smoothly into batters rather than the gritty sandiness left from granulated sucrose.

Dense cookies that resemble hockey pucks rather than lightly aerated treats point to insufficient rising agents or possible ingredient measurement errors, skewing the careful chemistry balancing sweetness, structure, and moisture. Check teaspoons and tablespoons used to ensure accuracy. Consider weighing out ingredients for the most precision. Take a fresh look at the leaveners used, increasing by ¼ teaspoon increments in following test batches if too dense until hitting the airy, sweet spot.

Hard, tough cookies that refuse to soften or crumble apart suggest overworked doughs and overdeveloping starches through extensive mixing. Use a gentler folding method after the initial creaming stage and mix in any chunky add-ins like chocolate chunks or nuts. The ideal consistency falls somewhere between stiff peaks like cake batter and shaggy loose dough that won't retain shape when scooped.

Overly crumbly and tender cookies can stem from ingredient omissions or substitutions, throwing off the careful ratios of binding agents that hold baked goods together. For example, swapping out whole eggs for whites eliminates fat and protein vital to chewy structure. Too much leavener leaves little base to support air pockets. Include some form of fat, whether butter, oil, shortening or white bean puree. Supplement with powdered milk, golden flax meal or psyllium husk to compensate for any missing proteins or gums.

Baked goods turning out overly sweet or saltier than expected points to potential issues in seasoning. Imprecise measuring leads to skewed outcomes, so always level off spoonfuls of sugar or salt, then check weights on a scale if adjusting recipe proportions. Humidity causes powders like sugar to compact, so sift first for true volumes. Taste doughs before baking and adjust as needed to prevent lackluster cookies masked behind cloying sweetness or harsh salt edge.

Uneven baking amongst cookie sheets results in simultaneously under and overdone treats with puzzling inconsistencies. Rotate pans front to back and switch racks midway for most even exposure relative to heating elements and fans. Insulated baking sheets prevent hotspots, while stoneware absorbs and then radiates warmth for crispier bottom crusts. Check oven temperature gauges or use an independent thermometer placed on the center rack to confirm the accuracy of settings.

That covers common issues arising in gluten-free cookies, from mixing methods to baking variables. Next up, in Chapter 8, we explore the decadent world of brownies and blondies. Do you crave a fudgy texture or a cakey crumb? We'll outline tips for achieving both ends of the spectrum using pantry staples along with creative additions like coffee, spices, citrus, and more to transform basic batters into next-level bakery quality indulgences. Delve into the chapter to take your bar cookie repertoire to the next level!

Storing Cookies to Maintain Freshness

A well-designed cookie tin easily aspires to become a prized family heirloom as the well-loved receptacle where freshly baked treats get tucked away from munching hands until appropriate dessert time rolls around again. Its sturdy construction withstands generations of use and washings in a rainbow of cheery hues. Snap closures keep contents contained and secure so cookies don't end up stale and crumbled remnants by the time your recipe testers return home from track practice ravenous for an afternoon snack.

Larger cookie cabins store dozens of rounds or rows of bars upright in neatly labeled glass jars with sufficient spacing between them to avoid squishing and smearing delicate glazed surfaces. Smaller handheld tins hold a modest sampling perfect for gifting colorful assortments to family and friends. Mini single-serving tins allow for self-rationed nibbles spread out over a leisurely week rather than ravaged right away in one shameful sitting. Or reusable BPA-free plastic totes stand up to everyday toting back and forth for easy grab-and-go cookie convenience.

Double up your storage potential with an expandable multi-tiered style basket unit custom-designed to hold dozens upon dozens of individually wrapped cookies, bars, and hand pies to tide you over from one epic baking bonanza to the next. Felt dividers prevent neighboring treats from sticking together into a coagulated lump. The whole apparatus folds down into a deceptively compact stack for closet storage after you empty each compartment.

Take care to let cookies cool completely to room temperature before packaging up. Fresh from the oven, steam and heat cause condensation, leading to unpleasant sogginess seeping into crisp structures. Fifteen to thirty minutes resting on racks renders cookies firm enough for storage duty. Use this window of time to create gift bags with personalized name tags and ribbons to compliment specific recipients. Just don't add as an embellishment until the day of gifting so the package decorations don't wilt and fade over prolonged storage spans.

Stash extra homemade cookie dough balls or slice-and-bake logs well wrapped in plastic in handy portions right inside your freezer. Let thaw in the refrigerator overnight before baking into enticingly warm treats ready right at after-school snack time. Label cookie dough for freezing with type, baking temperature, and approximate baking duration needed. Such helpful teens can take over kitchen duty and pitch in surprising siblings fresh from swim practice with a favorite nostalgic childhood treat from simpler times.

Cookies lacking substantial moisture, like meringues and biscotti, boast exceptionally long shelf lives, upwards of a month when properly stored. Take advantage by preparing big batches during free weekends and then parceling them out over weeks as easy dessert additions to weekday dinners. Simply stored in canisters on countertops, their low water activity and high sugar content prevent spoiling without the need for refrigeration or freezing.

Guard against early cookie spoilage by protecting boxes and tin contents from ambient moisture and humidity in pantries or cupboards. Desiccant packets like those found in packaging shoeboxes, beef jerky, vitamin bottles, and electronics boxes come in handy for absorbing environmental moisture that causes ingredients to clump and harden prematurely. Toss one or two into each airtight cookie container as added insurance so your handiwork stays crispy and chewy for the duration.

Freezing extends homemade cookie shelf life exponentially from days into months, though execution requires care. Allow cookies to cool completely after baking, then place desired serving portions inside zip-top freezer bags or airtight plastic containers with as much air squeezed out as possible. Press flat before sealing to minimize air pockets and associated ice crystal development that leaves a stale, icy taste behind the thawing time. Include a sticky note inside detailing cookie type, preparation tips, and reheating instructions for whomever eventually defrosts your thoughtful frozen gift.

Be selective regarding which cookie types take well to freezing and storage over the long term. Dense cookies packed with chocolaty chunks like brownies and blondies freeze solidly into fudgy, frigid slabs. Allow to thaw slowly overnight in the refrigerator to prevent crumbling. The condensed milk and mini chocolate chips in chocolate crinkle cookies keep the batter moist after freezing. Nutty shortbread cookies avoid freezer burn thanks to naturally oil-rich ingredients providing sufficient coverage with less risk of water crystals piercing through.

Avoid freezing ultra-delicate cookies like French macarons, which absorb ambient humidity and lose structural integrity, collapsing into pasty sweet puddles upon thawing. Similarly, cookies like lace tuiles with detailed shapes imprinted risk emerging from the freezer battered and blurred beyond recognition. High moisture, no-bake refrigerator cookies turn mealy over time from trapped ice condensing with nowhere to evaporate once frozen solid. Save those cookie types for immediate fresh enjoyment the day of baking or brief storage at room temperature.

Seeking an oven-free way to re-crisp bagged cookies that have gone disappointingly soft? Simply tuck open bags into the microwave alongside a small bowl of water and zap for 20-second intervals. The ambient humidity released from the heated bowl essentially steams cookies back to crispy life without overcooking the centers, like direct reheating tends to cause. This clever trick can reclaim cookies from the brink of stale defeat when unexpected guests suddenly stop by while your baking ingredients supply runs low.

Whipping egg whites into lofty peaks looks and feels physically demanding yet rewards perseverant bakers with ethereally crisp cloud-like cookies. The process unfolds similarly to churning cream into butter, where sufficiently whisked egg whites transform from slimy transparent glops into snowy white pillowy mounds. Past the soft peak stage, stiff peaks form, clinging upright and slowly losing definition on whisk tips before collapsing into grainy, unattractive clumps if overwhipped. Halt mixing once peaks stand straight up with tips just starting to fold over for bake-ready meringues.

A perfectly baked and stored gluten-free cookie strikes an evanescent balance between satiny, crisp snap, immediately dissolving into tender sandy crumb against your tongue. Subtle sweetness coaxes out mystical flavors from humble pantry staples like vanilla's heady bouquet and cinnamon's smoldering zest. Textural intrigue arises from scattered mix-ins smuggling in crunchy cereal bits, chewy dried fruits, or communal chocolate chunks beckoning for equitable distribution with each bite. A homey aroma wraps around the kitchen, promising convivial moments shared over a humble yet exquisite hand-crafted cookie.

Chapter 8

Brownies and Blondies: Fudgy, Cakey, or Both

Nope! We're not referring to women's hair! Brownies are a fun type of snack common among folks worldwide. However, even some experts don't know how to bake it right! When it comes to chewy, fudgy, all-around incredible brownies, using the right ingredients and techniques is key. We'll explore the foundations for creating brownies with ultra-rich chocolate intensity and irresistible texture.

The Ultimate Fudgy Brownie

Our journey begins with unsweetened chocolate. This pure, concentrated cacao lends bold chocolate flavor without added sugar. Combining a full cup of unsweetened chocolate with one cup of brown sugar and half a cup of white sugar strikes an ideal balanced sweetness. The brown sugar contributes moisture and chew, while the white sugar lightens the crumb slightly. Sugar also helps emulsify the fat and liquid components.

For the liquid, a combination of brewed coffee and canola oil proves unbeatable. The coffee intensifies the chocolate's presence without overpowering it. Oil allows a more fudgy texture than butter alone would yield. After testing every ratio under the sun, using a one-third cup of coffee to half a cof up oil enables seriously fudgy brownies that still hold their shape when cut.

As for flour, all-purpose has just enough gluten for structure without toughening the treats. Almond flour lends a delightful nutty aroma and tender crumb. Using three-quarter cups of all-purpose and one-quarter cup of almond flour gives the best texture and rise.

Eggs provide moisture, structure, and lift. Two extra-large eggs whipped to a light, fluffy texture prevent the brownies from becoming dense and heavy. Beating the eggs properly makes all the difference.

In terms of mix-ins, nothing beats chopped walnuts and chocolate chips. Toasted walnuts offer a delightful crunch and buttery flavor that pairs perfectly with chocolate. About a half cup provides ample scattered walnut joy in each bite without weighing down the batter. Mini chocolate chips melt into pockets of gooey chocolate ecstasy. Adding a full cup allows chocolate in every single nibble.

With an arsenal of top-notch ingredients, proper technique transforms the batter into fudgy brownie magic. We'll explore vital tips and tricks along the journey from mixer to oven.

First, water baths are an essential secret weapon! Heating the melted chocolate, coffee, and oil gently together in a water bath prevents scorching and allows the mixtures to emulsify smoothly. Stirring constantly with a spatula, remove the bowl when an instant-read thermometer registers between 120°F to 130°F.

Next, whipped egg whites give an irresistible lift to the crumb. Using a stand mixer or hand mixer, beat the egg whites until frothy and beginning to hold soft peaks, about 2-3 minutes. Move swiftly so as not to overbeat.

In another bowl, beat the brown sugar, white sugar, and eggs together until thickened and pale yellow, about 5 minutes. This crucial step properly dissolves the sugar and adds air into the structure.

Switch to a flexible spatula and gently fold the chocolate mixture into the egg mixture just until combined. Sprinkle the flour and almond meal over the top and gently fold again until fully incorporated. Finally, fold in the egg whites, chocolate chips, and walnuts until just combined, being careful not to overmix.

For baking pans, nonstick aluminum pans produce the most consistent results. Metal conducts heat more evenly than glass or ceramic for ideal rising and crumb texture. Lightly grease the pans, even if using nonstick. This prevents sticking and creates a slight barrier, allowing magnificent lift along the edges.

Before filling the pans, preheat your oven to 325°F. This relatively low temperature allows the brownies to bake slowly, developing superior fudge appeal without drying or forming a crust. Fill the pans nearly to the top for ultra-thick and fudgy results.

Bake for 25-30 minutes, then test doneness by gently shaking. The edges should look set, while the middles still jiggle slightly. This underbaked fudge gelato-esque texture provides brownie nirvana.

Allow to cool completely before cutting if you can resist that long. Top with powdered sugar or vanilla ice cream. Then sink your teeth into the ultimate fudgy brownie bliss!

With the foundations forged, let's explore irresistible add-ins and swirls. Mixing various chunks, flakes, and ripples of flavor into our brownie base batters creates decadent desserts that dazzle the senses.

Take mint chocolate brownies, for instance. Adding a teaspoon of mint extract and two drops of green food coloring to the basic batter provides refreshing mint chocolate intensity. Breaking a peppermint patty into chunks and swirling it in creates irresistible pockets of velvety mint.

For turtles-inspired brownies, sprinkle a cup of chopped pecans over the batter along with a half cup of caramel baking bits before baking. The nuts toast to a delightful crunch, and the caramel melts into swirls of sweet buttery bliss.

Cookies and cream brownies burst with Oreo cookie crumbles, milk chocolate chips, and white chocolate chips swirled throughout a rich chocolate base. Breaking six Oreos into chunks and mixing them with the mini chips delivers cookie crumble joy in every bite.

Rocky Road brownies come loaded with mini marshmallows and chopped walnuts sprinkled over the top just before baking until melted and toasted. The marshmallows puff into sweet, pillowy bubbles while the walnuts add a delightful contrasting crunch.

Take s'mores brownies over the top by mixing mini marshmallows, chopped graham crackers, and milk chocolate chips into the batter. Top with more marshmallows before baking for the ultimate campfire classic without the campfire.

Speaking of s'mores, for a showstopping skillet brownie, mix mini marshmallows, chocolate chips, and roughly broken graham crackers into the batter. Bake in a well-greased 10 or 12-inch cast iron skillet. Top with more marshmallows in the last 5 minutes of baking. Serve bubbling hot with ice cream.

For PB&J brownies, swirl in peanut butter and your favorite jelly. Heat one-third cup of peanut butter with three tablespoons of jelly in the microwave at 30-second intervals, stirring until melted and combined to a ripple-able texture. Dollop blobs over the filled brownie pan and swirl through using a chopstick before baking.

Lemon raspberry brownies burst with brightness thanks to mixing in a tablespoon of lemon zest and half a cup of frozen raspberries along with substituting a quarter cup of fresh lemon juice for a quarter cup of coffee. Top with a lemon glaze if desired by mixing powdered sugar, lemon juice and zest.

Spiced Aztec brownies pack a punch with two teaspoons of Mexican chili powder, a teaspooof n cinnamon,a half teaspoon nutmeg, and cayenne pepper mixed into the batter, and a half cup of chopped dark chocolate. Top with melted dark chocolate, cayenne, and sea salt flakes.

Take chocolate cherry brownies over the top by using cherry juice in place of the coffee and mixing a cup of chopped bittersweet chocolate with a half cup of roughly chopped dried cherries into the batter. Divine!

And for the peanut butter chocolate lover, nothing beats swirling peanut butter cup buttercream over warm-from-the-oven brownies. Simply beat together peanut butter, powdered sugar, vanilla and enough milk to reach a spreading consistency. Spoon and swirl over brownies, then sprinkle chocolate shavings on them.

With your brownie foundations along with creative mix-in and swirl inspirations, you now hold the keys for conjuring up fudgy brownie magic sure to delight any crowd. But now, let's journey over to the lighter side of the tracks with sweet and chewy blondies.

Blondie Baking Bliss

While brownies rely on ultra-rich chocolate intensity, blondies celebrate sweet, buttery vanilla, brown sugar, and white chocolate flavors. We'll uncover the foundations for chewy baked bars bursting with brown sugar as well as inspired mix-ins to take the flavor factor over the top.

Our most decadent blondies yet start by creaming one and a quarter cups of packed brown sugar and one cup of butter until fluffy and pale brown. For an electric mixer, beat on high speed for 5 minutes. The prolonged whipping properly integrates air for maximum lift and chew factor.

Next, add two large eggs one at a time, followed by two teaspoons of Mexican vanilla for depth of flavor. Beat again after each addition until incorporated. Vanilla and eggs provide moisture and structure to balance the crisp sugar edges.

In another bowl, whisk together one and three-quarter cups of King Arthur Gluten Free Multi-Purpose Flour with half a teaspoon of xanthan gum, a quarter of a teaspoon of salt, and half a teaspoon of baking powder. This specially formulated blend lends the ideal protein balance for gluten free blondies with just enough lift yet dense, fudgy appeal. The touch of baking powder gives added rise and lightness.

Gently fold the dry mixture into the wet mixture by hand just until incorporated. Overmixing causes toughening, resulting in tooth-aching density.

Next, the mix-ins! For ultra chewy and gooey white chocolate blondies, fold in one and a quarter cups white chocolate chips. The abundance of melty white chocolate delivers sweet intensity in every bite.

Mix in a half cup of toffee bits and half cup of roughly chopped walnuts for a delightful crunch and butterscotch flavor contrast.

For pan prep, using an aluminum 8 by 8 inch baking dish lined with parchment paper allows cleanly lifting out the entire blondie slab after cooling. Nonstick spray ensures the parchment sticks in place.

Bake at 350°F for 22 to 25 minutes until the edges appear set and lightly browned, yet the middle still looks underbaked and jiggles slightly when shaken. This fudgy gelato-like texture provides the ultimate chewy blondie pleasure.

Allow it to cool completely before cutting if it is humanly possible to resist. Dust with powdered sugar for sweet vanilla billowy heaven. Serve with caramel swirl ice cream for total over-the-top joy.

Now that we have conquered the foundations of chewy butterscotch vanilla blondies, let's get creative with crave-able flavors. Just as with brownies, mixing in various add-ins, chunks, ripples, and drizzles takes blondies over the top.

For turtle pecan blondies, mix in a half cup of roughly chopped pecans along with half a cup of caramel baking bits to the batter before baking. The pecans toast to a wonderful crunch while the caramel melts into swirls.

Peppermint white chocolate blondies burst with crushed candy cane mixed into the batter along with white chocolate chips. Top with crushed peppermint candies for a festive flavor explosion.

Tropical blondies bask in the glory of mixing a quarter cup each toasted shredded coconut, chopped macadamia nuts, and half a cup of chopped dried mango into the batter. Top with an orange coconut glaze of powdered sugar, orange juice, coconut milk, and shredded coconut if desired.

Take honey peanut butter blondies over the top by swirling in peanut butter cup cookie dough. Simply mix together peanut butter, sugar, an egg, and enough gluten-free flour blend to form a thick dough. Dollop over the batter, swirl, and bake until the cookie dough sets. Magic!

For s'mores insanity, mix mini marshmallows, chopped chocolate bars, and broken graham cracker pieces into the batter along with the white chocolate chips. Top with more marshmallows before baking. Serve straight from the pan, bubbling hot with ice cream.

And for peanut butter and jelly blondies, melt your favorite jelly and peanut butter together to make a ripple mixture. Heat one third cup of peanut butter with a quarter cup of jelly, stirring frequently until melted. Swirl dollops over filled blondie pan. Bake until set for PB&J heaven.

Candy-coated blondies burst with swirled-in M&M's, Reese's Pieces, butterscotch chips, and toffee bits scattered over the top of a basic blondie batter. The candy melts into rivers of chocolate peanut butter joy.

Take blondies over the top with a dulce de leche swirl. Stir a quarter cup dulce de leche caramel sauce into sweetened condensed milk. Dollop this mixture over the batter and swirl for incredible gooey caramel ribbons throughout.

Wildberry white chocolate blondies simply sing thanks to mixing a cup of fresh mixed berries and half a cup of white chocolate chips into the batter. Dollop your favorite berry jam over the filled pan and swirl for fruity decadence.

With proper technique, along with creative mix-ins, swirls, and toppings, you can now conjure up both fudgy brownies and chewy blondies sure to impress any crowd. When only chocolate and sugar will cure a trying day or sweeten life's blessings, turn to brownies and blondies to lift your spirits. Fudgy, Cakey or Both" with a focus on achieving the perfect blondie texture:

As we learned, constructing chewy butterscotch blondies relies first on creaming brown sugar and butter to a fluffy, pale texture. This aerates the mixture for increased rise and light texture. But take care not to overbeat at this stage, or the over-mixed batter bakes up tough and toothachingly dense. Ideally, we aim for maximum lift while retaining fudgy appeal.

Finding this sweet spot requires learning the nuances of properly creaming butter and sugar. When done by hand, maintaining a smooth, rapid rhythm with your strongest arm keeps the mixture light rather than overworking into greasiness. Those first tempting wisps of fluff actually indicate an imminent breakdown. Stop just as the color lightens before curdling.

By machine presents its own perils. Scraping down the bowl repeatedly during beating prevents uneven incorporations, which bake unevenly. But resisting that temptation to walk away allows destructive overbeating. Relying on mixers with bowl scrapers eliminates this dilemma. For others, remaining vigilant for the 5 minutes of creaming while distracting yourself elsewhere leads to disappointment later.

The type of sugar also greatly impacts texture. While ordinary white granulated sugar works fine, the ultimate chew factor unlocks by using brown sugar. The moisture creates bubbles released as steam during baking for increased rise. Dark brown sugar gives even more moisture and deeper flavor. Combining both light and dark brown offers an ideal compromise, adding moisture without overpowering flavor. The sumptuous butterscotch essence permeates each bite.

Always use packed brown sugar measured firmly to prevent collapse and ensure accurate ratios for the recipe. Packing the measuring cup squares off the sugar without gaps, allowing precision. Use fingertips to press firmly into all corners without compacting completely solid. Level by sweeping a straight edge across the top, removing the excess.

Never attempt substituting powdered sugar in place of brown or white granulated sugars. Powdered sugar contains cornstarch, preventing proper creaming ability and moisture balance. The batter bakes up overly dry and toughened, resembling concrete more than tender treats. Likewise, honey and other liquid sweeteners throw off recipe ratios, detrimentally impacting texture. Always use measured packed brown sugar for ideal lift and chew.

In terms of butter, high-fat content ensures flakiness while avoiding greasiness. The higher fat content incorporates more tiny air pockets, leavening blondies to great heights. Using a lower-grade butter containing more water results in a shorter, denser texture with increased greasiness. Less pleasantly, budget butter also lends subtle meaty or sour flavors.

Quality European-style butter provides an exponentially enhanced experience over ordinary American grocery store varieties. Their higher fat ratios and slower churning method capture more air, distributing it evenly throughout the butter block. Treat yourself to a mellow, sweet flavor with nutty aromas, which will pleasingly enhance any recipe.

Cultured butter, often sold in European style, undergoes fermentation by live active cultures, producing its distinctive tang. This longer processing method changes molecular bonds, providing superior water dispersion and flakier properties. Using cultured butter in creaming helps aerate the batter while introducing depth of flavor.

Take care to soften butter properly before creaming. Either set out covered overnight or microwave at 15-second intervals until malleable but not melted. Attempting to cream cold solid butter containing an overly high ratio of water produces a dense tough texture with visible butter pieces speckled throughout. Properly softened butter blends smoothly with sugar for a chewy supple wonder.

Another vital component consists of eggs added after creaming butter and sugar. Eggs provide additional lift by incorporating air into the blended batter. Take care of cracking eggs properly before adding them to prevent potentially contaminating them with bacteria-laden shells.

Choose eggs approaching room temperature by setting out ahead for 30 minutes. Cold eggs from the fridge do not foam up as readily to their fullest rising potential. Room temp eggs whip up fluffier, increasing lift once incorporated into other ingredients.

Crack eggs by firmly tapping the rounder side against a hard, flat surface such as the counter, separating the shell cleanly into two halves. Gently pull apart a small container to catch any errant shell pieces and the valuable egg itself in case of an accident. Carefully pour the egg back and forth between shell halves, allowing the egg white to drag any clinging shell down with it into your container.

Those proficient at cracking and separating eggs swiftly with one hand against an edge risk contaminating the rest of the recipe with errant shell pieces. Better safe than sorry. Or salmonella poisoning from consuming raw eggs with shell shards.

Individual sensitivities to consuming raw eggs varies greatly between people and egg sources. Pasteurizing eggs before baking provides added insurance for vulnerable groups by heating gently to destroy potential bacteria before use.

Create your own pasteurized eggs safely with an accurate candy or deep fry thermometer. Place cold whole eggs still in their shell into a saucepan and cover with cold water by one inch. Heat over medium, stirring gently until the water reaches 140°F degrees. Maintaining this temp for 3 minutes kills bacteria yet avoids curdling eggs. Remove promptly afterward and submerge eggs in an ice bath to prevent overcooking until needed for recipes.

Eggs lend additional lift by whipping trapped air into light, fluffy, foamy textures. Creating meringues and eating completely raw bears the highest risks for contamination. But gently whipping whole eggs just until combined before blending into batters raises the potential safely.

Whip eggs in a separate container rather than directly inside the stand mixer bowl used for creaming butter and sugar. Traces left behind alter the foam-stabilizing properties of fresh egg whites. Use scrupulously clean stainless steel, glass or copper bowls free of residue or smells, along with whisk or mixer attachments to prevent inhibiting foaming.

Adding some or all egg whites whipped separately to soft or medium peaks and then gently folding them into the completed batter right before baking increases rise and chewiness dramatically. This builds an interconnected web of air pockets releasing as the egg proteins set during baking. But overdoing may cause collapse. Follow recipe guidelines for best results.

Properly whipped eggs lend increased lift and moisture, creating the signature chewy tender crumb blending wonderfully with brown sugar's molasses notes in blondies while avoiding dryness or dense texture. Finding the right balance between density and airy lightness relies first on accurate measurements using weight rather than cups or spoons. Failure to accurately level ingredients by not using precise tools causes textural troubles later.

Digital kitchen scales provide the easiest, most reliable form of weight-based measuring for baking recipes. Simply place your mixing bowl on the scale and reset to zero after adding each ingredient. No adjustments are needed, regardless of altitude. Those comfortable with imperial units can still take advantage of precision weight ratios while ignoring the numbers on screen.

Cups work reasonably well for liquids, and semisoft ingredients are easily patted down into them. But dry granulated or powdery ingredients must be carefully spooned in and then leveled off by sweeping a straight edge across the top, removing excess material without compressing. Packing down dense ingredients like brown sugar measured by cups requires a special hand-packing technique as previously described, to achieve proper density.

Measuring spoons come in standardized sets calibrated for accurate portioning. Level ingredients precisely using the straight-edge method. Overfilling causes excess, which prevents recipes from working correctly by throwing off the ratios.

For wet, sticky ingredients like honey, peanut butter, or molasses, spray measuring cups with nonstick spray first. The tiny layer prevents sticking to edges, allowing contents to slide out cleanly. If needed, use a flexible spatula to guide the last bits out while avoiding scraping down into the cup permanently. Rinsing and drying immediately afterward keeps them crisp and easy to use next time. Consider buying a second set just for sticky situations.

Follow recipe instructions carefully, whether using weight or cup measurements for any ingredients requiring special handling, like brown sugar. And always using measuring tools designed specifically for the kitchen provides reliability that traditional coffee scoops or plastic baby spoons lack.

Mixing all elements with care allows properly aerated batter to rise high in the oven, developing signature chewy centers with crispy edges in baked blondies. But precisely monitoring oven temperature proves equally important for ideal lift without drying.

All ovens differ in their true temperature compared to the setting dial. An oven thermometer placed inside while preheating reveals the actual operating temp. Start by preheating 25 degrees lower than the recipe states if it is running hot. Then, adjust longer bake times accordingly to prevent burning yet cook interiors completely.

Oven hot spots also greatly affect baking consistency from front to back and between racks. Rotate pans halfway during baking to even exposure. If one area burns repeatedly compared to the rest, this indicates a strong hot spot. Avoid using that area of the oven or rearrange racks to protect delicate items.

Insulate pans from the bottom oven heat by doubling up sheets of foil or placing them inside another pan. Allow airflow underneath by raising on a rack. This promotes even gentle rising heat from all sides rather than intense direct bottom heat, which overbrowns the bottom before the interiors finish baking.

Glass and ceramic pans retain heat longer, causing carryover cooking after removal from the oven. Check slightly sooner and allow extra standing time before cutting. Insulated pans and ceramic stones radiate ambient heat great for bread doughs but easily overbake delicate items.

Metal pans conduct heat quickly with no carryover effect. These work best for even gentle browning and lift. Line with parchment paper or use nonstick for easy release after cooling if desired.

For chewy centers with delicately crisped edges, underbake until just set in the middle with a slight jiggle when shaken. Carryover cooking firms up centers gently while retaining moisture without toughening the crumb. This also prevents unmelted ingredients like chocolate from potentially seizing up or hardening later as it cools. Allowing bars to finish setting on the counter develops fudge appeal.

The most crucial final step rests in cooling completely before cutting for clean slices that retain shape. Severing warm bars causes gooey centers to lose the structural ability to uphold their edges. The bars then glue themselves back together as a giant blob once cooling later anyway. Instant gratification gives way to disappointment.

Placing hot pans directly into the fridge or freezer shocks the abrupt temperature change towards cold while still gently baking internally from residual warmth. This contracts outside edges too quickly while insides remain fluid, damaging the texture and resulting in cakey spaces or hardened chunks once fully cooled instead of fudge centers.

Cool pans on wire racks, allowing air to circulate underneath, preventing steam condensation from damaging delicate crispy edges. Then, once fully cooled all the way through, bars easily slice cleanly, retaining their charming shapes to impress all lucky recipients with your thoughtfulness.

Adding delicious mix-ins like white chocolate chips, toffee bits, and nuts takes textural pleasure over the top. But properly incorporating them without damaging delicate rise and chew requires gentle handling. We will next explore secrets for blending in chunky add-ins without compromising delicate lift and crumb.

Chapter 9
Muffins: Portable Pleasures

Muffins represent convenient everyday indulgences relying on pantry staple ingredients transformed alchemically through mixing and baking into sublime portable breakfasts, snacks, or desserts. Their domed cake-like topping caps a tender, almost fluffy crumb generally flecked with goodies like fruit, nuts, or chocolate baked right in. Gluten-free bakers can easily replicate all our favorite muffin flavors, with recipe tweaks addressing structural and textural differences. We'll explore the wide, wonderful world of gluten-free muffins, including techniques for height, moisture, and that irresistible light cakey bite.

Muffins differ from other quick breads through a defining delicate texture plus a sweet profile. They strike a happy medium between ultra-rich butter-laden cookies and homey rustic bread loaves. Muffins feel fancy yet approachable simultaneously – perfect for breakfast on the go, an afternoon pick me up, or even gluten-free bakers can craft bakery-style muffins boasting gorgeous domed shape, balanced sweetness, built-in goodness from fruit/nut mix-ins, and that fluffy, almost cake-like consistency no crumbly dryness.

Gluten-free muffins do require more care, given the lack of stretchy binding protein that wheat provides. Gluten networks form the internal scaffolding, lending lift, structure, and moisture retention. Replacing some specialized ingredients plus pro tips yields sweet results, though! Let's review how to mix and bake featherlight yet flavored GF muffins.

Building Great Gluten-Free Muffin Batter
Gluten-free muffins start with our sturdy all-purpose flour blend combined with structure-boosting gums and leaveners. Butter or oil provides richness and moisture, while sweet elements like sugar or honey balance out. Eggs assist in binding and lifting while milk/dairy hydrates. After mixing our basic batter, stir through mix-in additions like fruit or nuts, which bake up throughout.Use your favorite multi-purpose cup-for-cup blend or DIY combo using rice flour, tapioca starch, sorghum flour and/or millet flour for gluten-free muffin recipes. Measure the flour precisely, packing it to ensure sufficient heft. Just ½ to 1 teaspoon of xanthan gum stabilizes GF batter magnificently, preventing tunneling or spreading. The key lies in activating it by mixing it into liquid early before adding other ingredients.

A couple tablespoons of tapioca or cornstarch further improve the binding, rise, and structure of gluten-free muffins. These leaveners cause muffins to dome upward beautifully, improve crumb texture, and initiate pleasing reactions to boost flavor. Use aluminum-free baking powder and baking soda options for best results. Butter or oil ensures muffins bake up tender while contributing buttery flavor and richness if desired; solid coconut oil works well, too.

Granulated/brown sugars or honey build cheery sweetness in gluten-free muffins, fuel leavening reactions, and promote browning. Maple syrup or molasses shine for accentuating flavors like pumpkin or gingerbread. Muffins crave moisture to prevent dry crumbs while adding nutrition, so eggs and dairy like milk/yogurt assist in binding and lift in some recipes. Sour cream or cream cheese can also help bind gluten-free batter.

As for textural accents, the options for tasty mix-ins feel limitless - stir through raisins, berries, nuts, chocolate chips, or anything that strikes your fancy via a spatula just until evenly incorporated throughout the thick muffin batter.Muffin magic emerges not just from proper measuring and mixing steps but also a few special tips any baker should remember for optimizing both the process and finished texture/flavor. Don't overmix – Blend GF muffin batters until just combined to avoid forming excess elastic gluten networks that then collapse unevenly. The batter looks slightly bumpy rather than silky smooth when done right! Allowing mixed muffin batter 5-10 minutes before scooping and baking allows gums/starches/leaveners to fully activate for better lift and shape. Baking in paper liners eases removal without sticking while preventing odd bottom crusting from some GF flours. For crunch fans, lightly oil or spray pans instead. Scoop batter into wells, heaping nearly full to allow for rise/spread room so muffins result with nicely rounded smooth tops. Given muffins brown most rapidly above oven vents when using multiple pans, rotate rack positions halfway through baking to even out doneness. Since muffins bake unevenly, poke a few in the center to confirm when evenly cooked through without wet doughy spots.   Gluten-free flours unleash such a broad spectrum of beloved flavors when baked up into muffins to consider for pairing options when selecting customized add-ins, spices, and topping combos to achieve your muffin vision. Sweet berries like cranberries, blueberries, raspberries, blackberries, and chopped strawberries all shine with your favorite all-purpose GF flour base, whipping up fruity muffins with vanilla, orange, almond extracts or cinnamon, then topping with crunchy raw sugar sprinkles. Tropical fruit banana muffins foster appeal by brimming with bananas plus pineapple/coconut/nuts/rum extracts or orange mango flavors boosted by lime zest to reflect bright sunny flavors. Cocoa powder or melted chocolate folds decadently into deep chocolate GF muffins, accented further with chocolate chips or dipped in silky ganache post-bake if desired. Toasting pecans, walnuts, macadamia nuts, or shredded coconut before stirring through richer caramel/butterscotch/maple muffin doughs amplifies texture fantastically. Savory cheddar herb muffins patterned after biscuits or dinner rolls work deliciously gluten-free thanks to flavor-packed add-ins like cheddar/chives/scallions, sun-dried tomatoes/basil/Parmesan or jalapeno/cheddar with corn kernels baked inside. Pumpkin pie spice, cinnamon sugar, gingerbread, apple pie, chai spice, or classic carrot cake spice profiles all translate marvelously into muffins capped with corresponding cream cheese frostings or streusel. More imaginative combos like cardamom lemon poppy seed, cinnamon pecan crunch, ginger pear crumble, and honey almond crunch unleash creativity.Using shared ingredient tips, precisely follow the steps for mixing together flexible master GF muffin batters, allowing customization through assorted mix-ins in order to achieve light, fluffy bakery-style domed muffins. Whisk together dry ingredients first - measure flour, xanthan gum, baking powder/soda, sugar, and salt into a medium bowl and mix to evenly distribute everything, sifting or breaking up any lumps. Blend wet ingredients like melted butter, milk, eggs, yogurt, and any liquid flavor extracts like vanilla in a separate bowl, whisking until fully emulsified. Combine the egg mixture with the dry ingredients gently just until blended with small flecks remaining visible rather than thoroughly incorporated. Gently stir any add-in nuts, fruit or chocolate throughout the thick batter, distributing chunks evenly. Cover the batter and allow resting 5 minutes before baking in order to fully activate leavening and structure. Portion generously into oiled muffin pan wells, bake, then enjoy fresh hot muffins soon drizzled with a schmear of jam or honey butter. Some mix-in combinations offering guaranteed success include lemon blueberry with tart citrus zest and sweet, juicy berries, perhaps finishing with a sugary streusel topping. Another winner proves applesauce oatmeal muffins - cozy and comforting while lactose-free for sensitive diets thanks to creamy applesauce binding instead of yogurt or milk. Or try velvety pumpkin pie flavor studded with melty chocolate surprises in the batter, topping with maple glaze or whisked cream cheese frosting. Whether craving fruity brightness, chocolate decadence or old-fashioned spice cake flavor, GF flour foundations empower home bakers to indulge their every muffin whim, so never pass up perfect vehicles for baking smiles.

Chapter 10
Pancakes and Waffles: Breakfast Bliss

Rising with the sun and savoring a stack of steaming hot, fluffy pancakes or golden waffles is one of life's great simple pleasures. Long a beloved morning tradition, pancakes, and waffles carry the promise of warm comfort, wholesome ingredients, and a sweet start to the day. And in the vast realm of baking freed from gluten, pancakes, and waffles reign supreme. These humble classics present some of the most satisfying challenges to recreate, dazzle, and improve upon sans gluten. Unlock the secrets to mixing, cooking, and crafting flawless gluten-free pancakes and waffles and you will be rewarded with bliss in each and every bite.

Reimagining pancake and waffle recipes can overwhelm any conscientious baker. The prospect of fickle flours, gums, and binding agents is daunting indeed. Fear not. While we may lack that springy wheat foundation, devotion to details and fine-tuning ratios of ingredients will allow us to build a strong base that ensures airy, stable pancakes and waffles. Let's explore some key steps to mixing and cooking stellar gluten-free pancake batter along with fixing any flaws.

Selecting flours and starches to mimic wheat gives structure while accommodating taste and texture poses the first obstacle. Breakfast Bliss", focusing on making light and fluffy waffles:

Making Light and Fluffy Waffles

When it comes to waffles, texture is everything. We desire waffles that walk the line between a crispy golden exterior and a tender, fluffy interior. Waffles should showcase a complex contrast of textures that mirrors the peaks and valleys of their iconic shape. Achieving this with gluten-free flour presents difficulties, but with strategic mixing methods and a carefully balanced batter, we can craft waffles that are ethereal yet substantial.

Our choice of flours and starches forms the framework that gives rise to lofty waffles. Whole grain flours like sorghum, millet, and brown rice flour supply earthy flavors, nutrition, and binding abilities but can yield dense results without assistance. Combining roughly equal parts whole grain flour, starch, and an accent flour proves optimal for lightness and structure. Cornstarch or tapioca starch lends crispness and promotes rising, while delicate flour like oat or superfine brown rice flour introduces tenderness. The inclusion of xanthan or guar gum stabilizes the batter, while a leavener gives an added boost.

Now, we must properly hydrate our dry mixture to form a smooth, pourable batter. Striking the right liquid-to-flour ratio is imperative, and it should be around 1 1/4 cups liquid per 1 cup of flour blend. Liquids with higher protein and fat, like milk or buttermilk, improve the batter's ability to trap delicate air bubbles. For flavor's sake, I adore using full-fat coconut milk, which imparts the subtle sweet essence of coconut. Eggs serve a vital role, allowing structure to form and contributing richness. Though two eggs often suffice, I endorse adding an extra yolk or two for a supremely decadent, almost custard-like base. Do exercise restraint from overbeating once ingredients are combined to preserve the batter's capacity to rise.

Armed with a well-balanced batter, we foray into the theatrical stage of cooking, where technique guides the final texture. I cannot overstate the importance of allowing your batter ample time to hydrate and relax. Simply let the mixed batter rest 20-30 minutes, which permits the flours to soften and starches to expand. The batter's viscosity will be reduced, improving flow and stackability. Before cooking, give the batter a gentle stir to reincorporate ingredients, but stop before overdeveloping gluten. Lightly oil your hot waffle iron, only filling each quadrant about two-thirds with batter. This leaves room for rising. Close the lid gently and anticipate magic unfolding. Peak after 3-5 minutes, then continue cooking to deeply brown and crisp the exterior.

Fresh out of the iron, waffles will glisten with a delicate crunch, giving way to a faintly sweet, nourishing interior. You'll note traces of vanilla and brown sugar amidst prominent grain flavors. Each fork-pierced bite bursts with contrasting sensations of crisp exterior versus fluffiness within. Topped with whipped coconut cream and maple syrup, this gluten-free waffle transports you, however briefly, to a blissful state. Its beauty lies in elegant simplicity, concealing the care applied to achieve loft and lightness. For this moment, little else matters beyond savoring a thoughtfully crafted waffle in good company.

Though technique proves vital, there exists some room for creativity in gluten-free waffle recipes. Whole grains like teff, sorghum, millet, or buckwheat add multidimensionality, while nut flours contribute richness. Consider adding a touch of almond or pistachio flour for a more indulgent route.

Infusing batter with bold flavors via spices, zests, extracts, or mix-ins like chocolate or fruits amplifies interest. Drizzle batters with melted chocolate or swirl in cherry compote or lemon curd for dazzling effects. Top finished waffles with anything from whipped cream to ice cream, butter, fruits in syrup, chocolate spreads, caramel, honey, or savory ingredients.

Waffles present a prime canvas for creative expression and reinterpretation. For special occasions, craft a stunning waffle bar with an array of housemade toppings and let guests build their own creations. Offer an assortment of flavored whipped creams, ice creams, fresh-cut fruits, chocolate and caramel drizzles, sprinkles, crushed nuts or candies, and other tempting treats. Allow sweet freedom of expression to match the freedom gluten-free waffles provide.

Chapter 11
Cakes: Layers, Loaves, and More

Baking luscious, layered gluten-free cakes presents some unique challenges compared to traditional baking. Without the elastic structure provided by gluten, achieving tender, fluffy layers that hold together can seem downright magical at times. Many bakers encounter issues like dense, gummy textures, uneven rising, cracking, and overly dry crumbs. Have no fear! With the proper ingredient substitutions and baking techniques, you can conjure up cakes that are so moist and decadent that no one will believe they are gluten-free. This chapter unlocks the secrets to heavenly layers by illuminating how alternative flours behave, how binding agents boost structure, and how proper mixing and baking steps prevent flaws. You'll learn to adapt everything from airy genoise sponges to rich pound cakes that dazzle the senses and melt in your mouth.

When I first started tinkering with gluten-free cakes, my initial attempts were, shall we say, less than stellar. I pulled my first cake out of the oven eagerly, only to watch the center collapse into a soggy heap. My next try emerged dense and sunken like a brick. Batch after batch ended up overbaked yet still moist to the point of being gummy.

Baking Without Bounds

I nearly resorted to tossing my precious alternative flours out the window! Thankfully, with trial, error, and persistence, I finally cracked the code on luscious gluten-free cakes. In my journey to lighter, fluffier layers, I tested different flour ratios extensively, played with binding agents, and analyzed moisture levels - all seeking that perfect tender yet stable crumb. While the science of gluten-free baking can seem daunting, don't let that intimidate you. We'll explore all the must-knows in this chapter so you can skip the guesswork and head straight to baking magic.

Ingredient Substitutions

When embarking on your gluten-free cake adventure, substituting the right ingredients is essential for both flavor and structure. We'll navigate the diverse options for alternative flours, binding agents, leaveners, fats, and more. Since gluten-free flours lack gluten's elastic networks, we must make up for that missing structure through strategic ingredient choices.

Gluten-Free Flour Options

Gluten-free flours vary widely in taste, texture, protein and starch content. Some mimic wheat more closely, while others provide uniqueness all their own. Outside of personal taste preferences, the protein and starch levels determine how flours can augment structure in gluten-free baking. Higher protein flours help achieve rise and bind batter, while higher starch flours offer tenderness. Blending flours balances these qualities. Here are some top contenders:

Almond flour naturally contains no gluten and lends a pleasant, nutty richness perfect for cookies, quick breads, and some cakes. With mainly protein and healthy fats, almond flour can lead to dense results without sufficient starch flour to offset the protein load. For the most tender results, pair almond flour with lighter options.

Buckwheat flour offers a distinct, earthy flavor and soft crumb. The protein content can help bind the batter, while the starch fosters moisture and lift. Combined with additional light flours, it yields a great cake texture. Those sensitive to buckwheat's assertive taste may prefer other neutral options. Some find mixing with mild flours allows buckwheat's benefits without overwhelming flavor.

Coconut flour boasts an ultra-crispy, coconut-esque bite. With abundant fiber, it requires exponentially more liquid than other flours, which can make balancing the structure tricky. For coconut flavor without as much soaking up of moisture, use coconut flour sparingly in blends. Increase eggs and liquid to account for coconut flour's thirsty qualities.

Garbanzo bean flour (chickpea flour) generates superb lift and springy texture in gluten-free baked goods. Made from nutrient-packed garbanzo beans, it supplies a subtle bean flavor that plays well with vanilla, cocoa, spices, and citrus flavors. With higher protein than many gluten-free flours but lower fat than nut flours, it strikes an ideal balance for cake structure. Boost garbanzo bean flour with gums or starches.

Millet flour contributes a mild corn-like taste, velvety crumb, and helpful binding for sturdy layers that won't crumble. Similar protein content to all-purpose flour makes it a handy addition for improving the risen structure without a strong flavor profile. The tiny seeds offer a healthy dose of nutrients like magnesium, phosphorous and fiber. Because millet flour has less surface area compared to finley ground offerings, it can create a gritty texture if overused.

Preparing the Pans

Before we delve into mixing methods, let's discuss optimal cake pans for gluten-free success. This step may seem trivial, but using appropriate bakeware prevents many pitfalls. Without giving batter ample space to spread evenly and rise, you may end up with odd dome shapes, peaking, cracking, or uneven textures.

 Round pans measuring at least 2 inches high with straight rather than tapered sides work best. This prevents doming, where the center balloons are higher than the edges. Choose pans in sizes like 8x2 inches, 9x2 inches or 10x2 inches for flexibility based on the recipe's specifications. These dimensional ratios help layers bake evenly no matter what size you select. Pans that are overcrowded or too shallow lead to peaking or overflowing. If using novelty-shaped pans like hearts, use a size bigger than the recipe's round pan volume to allow ample room.

In terms of materials, basic aluminum pans conduct heat well for even layers but can cause darker color on crusts. Insulated or double-layer pans moderate this effect for paler exteriors but may require slightly longer bake times. Nonstick coatings ease release. Avoid glass or ceramic pans, which retain heat and can overbrown crusts. Warped or dented pans yield irregular textures, so use pans that are in good shape.

Always properly grease and flour pans or line the bases with parchment paper rounds. This prevents sticking that foils pretty layers and causes tearing. For greasing, use solid shortenings, butter, or nonstick sprays without added flour. Rub the fat thoroughly over the entire inner surface and just up the sides. A thin scrapable coating works better than blobs. After greasing, a gluten-free flour dusting helps layers cleanly release - tap out any excess.

Instead of greasing and flouring, parchment rounds save time and minimize sticking just as well. Trace bottoms of greased pans onto parchment, then cut out circles to fit bases perfectly.

Mixing Methods

Gluten-free batters require specific mixing techniques for optimal texture. We'll outline ideal methods from creaming butter to whipping egg whites when baking your next masterpiece layer cake or everyday snacking loaf.

The classic creaming method whips solid fat into fluffy incorporation before adding the dry and wet elements separately. Typically used for tender cakes and cupcakes, creaming incorporates air for a lift while coating flour particles in fat to limit gluten development. For our purposes, coating the flour maximizes moisture retention and rise. Granulated sugar works best for a fine, smooth crumb. After creaming the fat and sugar, add eggs, milk, liquids, or yogurt before gently stirring in the dry mixture alternately with liquids.

Foam cake methods prioritize whipping eggs and sugar first. After emulsifying the combination into a thick, aerated foam, the batter gets gently folded together, leaving those bubbles intact. Angel food cake follows this technique, which translates perfectly to our gluten-free agenda since the whipped eggs act as the structure builder instead of gluten. After meringuing the eggs and sugar, gently fold in flour, milk, or cream, melted fats, extracts, and spices at the end. Deflate the batter as little as possible.

The quick bread method quickly stirs together all ingredients without whipping steps. Typically employed for fast treats like muffins or loaves, it develops less rise than traditional methods. Binding agents become particularly key. The straightforward mixing minimizes handling that can overwork gluten-free batters. Advanced bakers may favor mixing some or all of the dry ingredients before adding liquids for ultra-tender crumb. This technique limits the activation of starches and gums that occur with excess stirring.

Batter Consistency

Depending on the desired results, gluten-free cake batters require different textures, from thin, pourable mixes to thick, scoopable doughs. Batters with higher liquid levels flow to fill pans easily and yield moist, even textures but compromise height. Thicker batters hold their shape better, achieving maximum rise with sometimes denser, more compact crumbs. Finding the right ratio depends on your priorities and chosen mixing technique.

For foam cakes, a thin pour is ideal as incorporating too much air deflates volume. Creaming and quick bread methods can handle thicker, spoonable consistencies since overly lean batters make cohesion difficult without ample starches or binding agents. As you add ingredients, evaluate the batter appearance and texture frequently. Scrape the sides and bottom of the bowl well when mixing. If too dry, batters clump on beaters, whereas too thin leaves wet residue streaking the bowl. Observe how the batter sits after pouring. Properly mixed batters should slowly smooth out in one steady puddle rather than separating.

Baking Tips

Preparing to bake your masterpiece cake requires forethought in oven conditions. Rushing steps lead to disasters like fallen centers, cracked domes, soggy interiors, or volcanic overflowing. Let's review best practices.

Always allow oven racks to fully preheat before baking for even heat distribution. Most standard or convection ovens work wonderfully with proper positioning for gluten-free cakes. Place layers towards the center of ovens, away from intensely hot rear heating elements or uneven fronts. Turn the pans 180 degrees midway through to even rise on all sides. Tests show pan rotations are not necessary in convection modes, so simply avoid edge placement.

Set oven temperatures accurately as gluten-free batters bake faster and more intensely. Invest in a reliable oven thermometer if unsure of calibration. Starting with correct temperatures prevents scrambling when over-browning occurs early, or cakes rise too slowly. Standard temps between 325-350F suit most balanced batters. Higher protein recipes bake faster due to greater binding, so they begin lower, around 300F. Very delicate egg-leavened recipes do best starting at 375F and then reducing heat to set structure.

Always watch layers carefully near finish times and do not rely solely on timers. Test doneness by pressing lightly at the edges or shaking pans gently. When it springs back slightly without visible indentation, it will cleanly pull away from the sides with no stuck bits. Use your best judgment - moist crumbs that jiggle more reflect underbaking, whereas firm, formed peaks signal overkill. Err on the side cautious side. You can serve a cake that's slightly underdone or use a longer cooling period before frosting, but no recourse exists for over-darkened hockey pucks!

Chapter 12

Frostings and Glazes: Sweet Toppings

Ah, frosting, the sweet embrace that takes a humble cake or cupcake from plain to party-ready in mere moments. Whether swirled sky high drizzled delicately, or simply spread smoothly across a cake layer, a good frosting can make or break your confectionary creation. Glazes, too, add that last touch of glossy goodness.

In this chapter, we'll explore easy homemade frosting options to dress up your gluten-free desserts. We'll also cover glazes from chocolate to lemon and everything in between. Consider it your complete compendium of crowning confection glory. Grab a spatula, and let's get started!

Making Basic Frostings

When I first started gluten-free baking, frosting felt tricky. So many recipes called for a magical "X cups confectioner's sugar" that I simply didn't have on my pantry shelf. After discovering powdery replacements like arrowroot and tapioca flours, I finally unlocked the secret code. Now, whipping up frosting feels like a breeze.

While specialty stores offer pre-made gluten-free frosting options, I find homemade allows me to control textures and flavors. It is not overly sugary, sweet, or too stiff to spread, but just right for any occasion. With a little trial and error, you'll soon find your own ideal consistency too. The base of butter and powdered sugar gets jazzed up with everything from cocoa powder, citrus zest, berries, spices, and beyond.

When gearing up to make the frosting, allow your ingredients—especially the butter—to come to room temperature. This helps everything incorporate smoothly. If pressed for time, soften butter quickly in the microwave with short 10-second bursts, checking often to prevent melted mush. Gather electric beaters, a spatula, piping tips if decorating, and extra bowls if mixing custom colors.

Let's explore some favorite fail-proof recipes, starting with a versatile vanilla base:

Classic Vanilla Bean Frosting

My tried and true vanilla frosting has a smooth, spreadable texture and rich vanilla bean speckles. For cupcakes or layered cakes, I use an offset spatula to generously coat sides and tops. Paired with chocolate cakes or spice cookies, vanilla balances other intense flavors. Adjust sweetness to taste with more or less powdered sugar. Splashes of milk or cream also thin thickness. Mix in berries or citrus zest to complement different desserts. And skip any artificial flavorings or food coloring—this one lets pure vanilla shine.

For birthday parties through backyard barbeques and beyond, this versatile vanilla crowns any gluten-free confection. Enjoy plain with champagne cupcakes or chocolate sandwich cookies, or spice it up with cinnamon on snickerdoodles. It pipes perfectly into flowers atop banana bread or swirls elegantly onto coffee cakes. Even sandwich a scoop inside whoopie pies for a creamy surprise. No matter the occasion, this frosting always fits.

Cream Cheese Frosting

What would carrot cake or cinnamon streusel coffee cake be without rich cream cheese frosting? That tangy creaminess perfectly offsets sweet cake and tart fruit fillings. Luckily it comes together just as easily without gluten. My trick? Tangling both brick-style regular cream cheese and honey-whipped varieties to build a lush texture. Softening at room temperature helps too—no fridge-cold chunks here. I beat the butter first before blending both cream cheese types to fully incorporate. Scrape down sides as needed to eliminate any lingering bits during mixing. The resultant frosting stays creamy but not runny and spreads smoothly but not stiffly.

Besides slathering between cake layers or rosette atop cupcakes, cream cheese frosting makes other tasty appearances. I'll stir a scoop into gluten-free oat bake for a stuffed streusel effect. Pack it into thumbprint cookies for a surprise filling. It's even been known to transform leftover cornbread or a humble bowl of grits into an impromptu dessert. Drizzled creatively over nearly any baked good, sweet and tangy cream cheese frosting rarely meets its match.

Chocolate Silk Frosting

For certified chocoholics like myself, no dessert feels fully dressed without an intense chocolate frosting swirl. Dark and bittersweet or creamy and dreamy—it must emerge deeply chocolatey. This recipe combines semisweet chocolate and cocoa powder along with espresso powder for extra depth. I vigorously whisk the warm water mixture into sugar to dissolve completely before adding butter in chunks and then eggs slowly while beating. The resultant chocolate silk coats a spoon thickly with a subtle shine that firms up beautifully once chilled. Mousse-like texture but spreadable enough for filling and frosting cakes or cupcakes, it's the best of both worlds.

Smear between cake layers, frost generously onto cupcakes or serve heaped in a bowl with fresh strawberries for dipping. Drizzle artfully over brownies or pie wedges for some extra sweetness, too. Smooth into whoopie pie centers or stir a spoonful into mug cakes before microwaving. However you swirl, spread, or dollop this luscious chocolate frosting, bliss is sure to follow.

Fluffy Marshmallow Frosting

When only cloud-like fluffiness will do, this marshmallowy frosting fills the bill. Mimicking that classic jarred brand, many grew up with, it piles high yet spreads smoothly. Corn syrup lends a glossy sheen and structure for excellent stability. I use gelatin to set the mixture, which gets whipped furiously into a billowy blanket of sweetness. The process seems lengthy, but each step contributes to the final airy yet sturdy result. Have patience and resist any temptation to rush things—good things come to those who wait!

The effort pays off in slippery, smooth frosting ready-to-frost cakes or pipe skyscraper cupcake peaks. Pair with chocolate, yellow cake, and carrot cake—marshmallow meltiness feels festive on nearly any flavor. Stir into brownie batter before baking for extra ooey-gooey appeal. Thumbprint cookies gain an unexpected filling. Even vanilla wafers or graham crackers become instantly irresistible when sandwiched together with fluffy marshmallow frosting in between. However you use it, be prepared for requests for seconds and thirds of this crowd-pleasing topper.

Buttercream Bliss

Nothing epitomizes classic frosting like a tried and true buttercream. Utilizing a sugar syrup cooked to a soft ball stage ensures a smooth, spreadable consistency with enough structure to hold its shape. Once cooled, the syrup gets whipped furiously into creamy softened butter. Billowing into satiny submission, this European-style buttercream delivers rich flavor and stable performance every time. I love experimenting with infusing different ingredients into the finished frosting—almond extract and raspberry puree are current favorites. Lavender honey or orange oil also subtly perfume each lofty swirl.

The versatility of buttercream makes it an oft-used option in my kitchen. Cupcakes, cakes, truffles, whoopie pies—it rarely meets a confection unable to improve. Light yet lush, slick but not runny, this balanced buttercream glides smoothly over desserts from cookies to crisps effortlessly. Stir in melted chocolate or peanut butter for more flavors, too. However you choose to swirl or slather it, buttercream takes any bake to the next level.

Whipped Coconut Cream

Seeking a lighter dessert finish without skimping on richness? Say hello to whipped coconut cream. Blending the solids skimmed from chilled cans makes magic in minutes. A brief whiz in the stand mixer or a furious session with a hand blender transforms watery coconut milk into the ethereal topping. I sweeten modestly with powdered sugar, then splash in vanilla and a pinch of salt. Sky high peaks form, ready to pipe or dollop onto treats in need of some tropical refreshment.

Pair coconut cream clouds with plain cake or fruits for a simple yet sublime dessert. Go all out tropical by frosting banana bread or hummingbird cupcakes too. For more decadence, mix in cooled melted chocolate before whipping. The possibilities feel as endless as summer, thanks to easy whipped coconut cream. Keep a few cans chilling in the fridge, or stash some solids in the freezer so you're never more than minutes from frothy fruit and cake adornment.

With endless frosting and glaze options to try, your gluten-free desserts will never go bare again. In the next chapter on Pies and Tarts, we'll move to flaky, fruity favorites perfect for a sweet ending to any meal. From quick single galettes to towering multi-layer confections, get ready to become pie-proud using your newfound gluten-free skills. But for now, go pick your pleasure pairing above and start spreading sweet magic one treat at a time!

Fruit Glazes: Sweet, Shiny Finishes

Baking Without Bounds

When I crave a dessert with minimal fuss yet maximum sparkle, fruit glazes always fit the bill. Relying on the natural sweetness of ripe seasonal produce, these toppings add glossy finishes with just a few ingredients. I'll often whip up a simple glaze as cakes or loaves cool to amplify fruity flavors already present. Other times, contrasting fruits pair beautifully, too—think tart lemon over strawberry bread or sweet apricot on a berry galette. Endless flavor combinations keep things interesting all year long!

Beyond embellishing cranberry cakes, blueberry custards, or raspberry tarts, fruit glazes also upgrade humbler desserts exponentially. Drive plain doughnuts, sugar cookies, or cups of pudding from boring to brilliant with a delicate drizzle. Even pancakes, muffins, and crisps feel instantly fancier when crowned with glistening sweetness. Often quicker than frosting, glazes require less finesse, too making them my shortcut to sweet success.

When crafting fruit glazes, the possibilities feel as boundless as summer bounty itself. Apples, plums, cherries, berries, stone fruits, citrus—so many options! I'll often hit up local farms for whatever peaks perfectly that week, from fuzzy peaches to plump blackberries or zingy nectarines. Pain perdu, Dutch baby pancakes, and galettes all become Effortlessly elegant and topped with seasonal shine. Beyond utilizing fresh fruit straight, some glazes call for jam, preserves, or even ice wine reductions to concentrate vibrancy. Bottled juice sometimes makes appearances when aiming to stretch shelves a bit longer, too. I'll jazz up plain lemon glaze with thyme leaves or cinnamon sticks infusing gently as it simmers for extra dimension. Versatility remains key no matter which fruits find their way into my mixing bowl.

While most glazes don't require anything fancier than a saucepan, having a few special tools on hand lends convenience. I'll often pass cooked glazes through fine mesh sieves if any errant seeds or chunks linger to ensure ultimate smoothness. Mini ice cube trays make portioning and freezing extra glaze for later a breeze—perfect for pulling out months down the road when summer's bounty feels far away. And definitely invest in a few pairs of disposable pastry bags for easy drizzling onto completely cooled items. Nothing ruins a glossy finish faster than accidental melted slumps!

When ready to glaze, have treats fully cooled first—warm surfaces cause melting mishaps in minutes. Work swiftly and avoid retracing your steps to prevent build-up. Chill glazes briefly first for even better viscosity and heat tolerance if needed. And most glazes last only a few days stored covered before losing luster. Prepare to polish off your creations quickly for the best texture and taste!

Now that we're set up for success equipment-wise, let's explore some stellar fruit glaze recipes...

Luscious Lemon Glaze

Pucker up! This sunny favorite brightens everything it touches with spirited sweet-tartness. Only requiring lemon juice, zest, honey, and salt, it comes together in just minutes. I'll reduce the mixture slowly until it thickens to a nape consistency—coating the back of a spoon while still dripping off easily. The touch of corn syrup helps prevent rock solid freezing so it remains drizzle-ready even after a chill. For extra zing, spike with a splash of vodka or limoncello if making an adults-only version!

Beyond drenching lemon loaves, sugar cookies, and fruit tarts, creative uses abound for vivid lemon glaze. Stir a spoonful into lemon curd before spreading between cake layers or lining pie crusts for double brightness. Mix with Greek yogurt for a breakfast parfait topping or fruit salad dressing. Brush onto pan seared chicken breasts, add to baked Greek chicken, or use as a base for lemon chicken marinade. Even plain roasted veggies or weeknight fish feel decadent topped with a lemony coating. However you drizzle it, this glaze sparks crave-able complexity worth savoring again and again.

Maple Pecan Glaze

Buttery and sweet, this amber glaze evokes nostalgia with every spoonful. Nutty pecan flavor accents rich maple for a cozy, comforting appeal. I lean towards Grade B darker maple syrup for brooding caramel essence, which gets heightened by a splash of brown sugar. Toasting pecan pieces to golden brown enhances their warmth too, before getting whisked into the simmered glaze. A pinch of cinnamon or cardamom ties everything together for optimal autumnal allure. Though divine on pecan pies, maple cake, or apple buckles, the uses for maple pecan glaze extend way beyond dessert.

Get creative with savory touches, too, like pairing with squash casseroles, roasted Brussels sprouts, or even drizzled-over oatmeal. The nutty maple sweetness plays well amidst dinner's supporting players as much as starring solo over sweets. And since pecan trees rain bounty come late fall, this glaze helps use up the excess beautifully. We even bottle quarts of it some years as hostess gifts or holiday presents when abundance overflows. Almost smoky, perfectly sweet, with loads of cozy character, maple pecan glaze remains a repeat recipe well past Thanksgiving leftovers at our house!

Honey Ginger Glaze

Seeking spice and sweetness in ripe harmony? Enter honey ginger glaze. Crystalized ginger is slowly simmered into rich honey with fresh ginger for a double dimension. I'll add pinches of cayenne or black pepper sometimes as well if craving subtle heat. A splash of rice wine vinegar helps cut through the sweetness for a bright balance. The resultant ruby glaze sings with sweet and spicy essence, lending a slight peppery kick to everything it coats.

Beyond expecting familiar friends like gingerbread, carrot cake, or pumpkin pie, expand your glazing horizons with honey ginger too. Brush onto plain yogurt ice cream or bread pudding for some smoldering sweetness. Use to top squash fritters, stir into Asian dipping sauces, or mix with peanut or almond butter. Even humble biscuits, scones, and cookies feel instantly punched up and drizzled with this glistening crowd-pleaser. Roasted chicken or stir fry also shines with some spiced honey love. However, if you use honey ginger glaze, its complex character promises pops of sweet heat sure to satisfy.

Raspberry Amaretto Glaze

Some days, only double fruity decadence will do when it comes to dessert gilding. For those moments, turn to tart, bright raspberry spiked with almond liqueur's cozy essence. Simmering jam intensifies natural berry sweetness into sticky syrupy submission. Corn syrup stabilizes so it pours slickly, while almond extract boosts nuttiness if avoiding alcohol. I'll also add drops of rosewater for floral intrigue that romances baked goods. Painted atop tarts, scones, cakes, or crisps, this glaze stuns with fruity depth and rosy aroma.

Beyond expected berry and stone fruit pairings, get creative with amaretto-kissed raspberry. Use as a sauce for cheesecakes, custards, trifles, or panna cotta. Stir into whipped cream or ice cream bases for extra fruity decadence. Mix with Greek yogurt to top waffles or pancakes at brunchtime. Even humble bowls of oatmeal feel special when dressed up with this vibrant topper. However you put it to use, raspberry amaretto glaze promises playful sweetness ready to mingle with myriad morning, noon, or night menu items.

Dressed up with shiny sweetness, nearly any dessert feels somehow complete once glazed to glossy perfection. Whether opting for spirited citrus, heady spiced honey, buttery brown sugar, or juicy jammy reductions, vibrant flavor abounds. And talk about easy elegance from fruit at peak freshness! Before you know it, becoming a glazing pro will feel like second nature. So grab a squeeze bottle and start amplifying everything from plain cake to supersized pie with a custom creamy, fruity final touch made from scratch. The sweetest things in life are often the simplest, after all!

Chapter 13

Pies and Tarts: Flaky, Fruity Favorites

As the aroma of baked fruit and sugar wafts through your kitchen, nothing says comfort quite like a perfect homemade pie. From traditional apple and pumpkin flavors to inventive combinations featuring berries, stone fruit, and exotics like mango or guava, a good gluten-free pie relies first and foremost on a flaky, tender crust that can hold abundant fillings. After all, even the most fragrant, spiced interiors require sturdy yet short walls to encase their contents.

In my early days of gluten-free baking, I struggled with pie doughs that crumbled apart, tasted gritty from rice flour, or emerged from the oven tough and dry. Yet over years of trial-and-error, along with guidance from generous bakers willing to share their secrets, I've discovered simple tricks that now help me easily turn out golden, crisp crusts every time.

As you begin your own adventures in flaky pies, keep in mind that creating the perfect gluten-free crust requires paying attention to details many bakers overlook at first. From precise ingredient measuring to careful rolling techniques, small tweaks make all the difference for a tender texture and flavor throughout.

You'll also want to bear in mind not only traditional doughs featuring butter, shortening, or lard but egg wash glazes, blind baking, and other special finishing methods for truly professional-looking treats right from your home oven.

This opening section covers my go-to recipe, guaranteed to help even novice bakers turn out picture-perfect pies. I'll share my secrets for avoiding soggy bottoms, patching tears, and crimping decorative edges worthy of country fairs. We'll also explore shortcuts like using parchment paper and pie weights for blind baking multiple crusts ahead of time.

Making the Perfect Gluten-Free Pie Crust
From proper mixing and chilling techniques to gentle rollouts between two floured sheets of wax paper, you'll learn how to handle gluten-free doughs with care and respect their tenderness compared to traditional wheat versions. Most importantly, I offer plenty of make-ahead and freezing guidance since extra pie crust rounds prepared in advance make whipping together after-dinner desserts simple on busy weeknights.

So preheat your oven, don your apron, grab a rolling pin in hand, and let's discover the joy and aroma of turning out delectable gluten-free pies and tarts! Savory main dishes or sweet final course confections await your creativity and my simple, fool-proof crust that forms the foundation of it all. Just be sure to brush up on your lattice weaving first! Flaky, Fruity Favorites":

Fillings and Flavors For Fruit Pies and Tarts

When it comes to fillings for fruit pies and tarts, the possibilities are endless. From summer berries to winter squash, citrus to stone fruit, and tropical indulgences to down-home apples, every season offers inspiration for creative fillings between flaky crusts. Although fruit plays the starring role in these sweet or sometimes tangy fillings, additions like spices, spirits, nuts, and even cheese lend contrasting flavors and textures.

As you experiment with fruit fillings, keep in mind that water content varies widely across produce options. For example, juicy peaches, plums, and berries release more liquid than firmer apples or pears. Adjust thickener amounts accordingly so that your fillings are set up properly without either too much moisture leaking into the crust or overly stiff, gelatinous textures. For particularly wet fruits like ripe strawberries, precooking with a bit of cornstarch allows more precision in the thickening power. But for less watery ingredients, immediately mixing all components together raw provides plenty of flow and mingling.

Beyond adjusting for moisture, remain open to embellishing fruity fillings with spices like cinnamon, nutmeg, ginger, and cardamom or floral waters like rose and orange blossom. Vanilla provides a blanket of warmth as well, especially paired with peaches, apricots, and berries. Toasted nuts lend crunch and richness, while herbs offer savory contrast; my favorite is scattering a few thyme leaves over simmering apples or pears.

For those who indulge in spirits, a splash of brandy, bourbon, rum, or liqueurs like amaretto and Frangelico seamlessly blend into many fruit fillings. Or try experimenting with regional combinations like apples with Calvados, cherries with Kirschwasser, or blueberries with Chambord. Just take care not to overwhelm the palate if you choose to spike your fruity desserts.

Beyond flavorings, most fruit fillings benefit from added texture as well. Depending on the variety you select, mix in oats, streusel, crushed biscuits or sandy shortbread, shredded coconut, or crispy-baked nut pieces. Topping your pie or tart with crumbles, streusels, whipped cream, or ice cream incorporates even more tantalizing layers too. For a stunning presentation, artfully cut fruit arranged in beautiful patterns never fails to impress.

As we explore fruit fillings in more detail, keep seasonal availability and purchasing tips in mind, too. For most home bakers, fresh ingredients provide the best results. But during off months, frozen, canned, or dried produce can shine as well with proper treatment. Learning optimal storage methods also helps reduce waste and yields better texture once incorporated into your pastry masterpiece.

So, let's embark on a tour of fruit options aligned with the calendar! Discover my techniques for handling everything from fragile berries to hardy winter squash. Along the way, I'll share coveted recipes perfected over years of gluten-free baking for memorable pies and tarts you'll want to enjoy all year round.

Chapter 14

Crisps, Crumbles, Cobblers, and Buckles

Fruit-based desserts are a joy to make and eat, especially when warm out of the oven on a cool evening. The sweet-tart flavors of peak summer berries and fall orchard fruits pair beautifully with a lightly sweetened, buttery topping in crisps, crumbles, and cobblers. And the humble buckle offers old-fashioned goodness from simple pantry ingredients. Gluten-free flours lend themselves well to these homey treats. Let's explore techniques and ingredient options to create crispy-crunchy, tender, and bubbly gluten-free toppings over luscious fruit fillings.

For fruit crisps and crumbles, your goal is a lightly sweet, crispy-crunchy topping to contrast the fruit filling's texture. Gluten-free flours won't form as much gluten, so mixing flours adds both structure and flavor. Bob's Red Mill or King Arthur Baking 1-to-1 gluten-free flour mixes are easy starters. Some crisp recipes use almond flour or almond meal, which contributes flavor and crunch. For a lighter texture, try superfine brown or white rice flour with tapioca starch. Corn flour or masa harina also add Character, and Toasted quinoa flakes offer nuttiness. Whatever flour blend you choose, incorporating cold butter is key for creating crispy crumbs when baked.

Baking Without Bounds

I prefer chilling the dry ingredients before adding the butter – the colder, the better to coat butter cubes before cutting them into the flour. Using your fingers, two forks, or a pastry cutter, break up the butter into hazelnut- to pea-sized crumbles encapsulated in flour. Avoid overworking into a dough. Then stir in any additional ingredients like sugar, spices or nuts.

For the fruit component, you want the texture to come through. For berries and stone fruits like peaches, nectarines or apricots, a quick roast heightens the fruit's flavors and helps release juices. For apples and pears, sliced thin to medium thickness retains some bite after baking. Regardless, taste the fruit mixture before adding sugar or spices to suit the natural sweetness and tartness of that day's harvest. Freezing fruit ahead for winter crisps and cobblers imparts beneficial textural changes. Cell walls expand and break down from ice crystal formation, softening the fruit once thawed and heated during baking.

To assemble crisps and crumbles for baking, spoon fruit into a buttered baking dish like a 9-inch round, 8-inch square or 11x7-inch rectangle until lightly mounded, about 2 inches deep. Distribute the topping evenly over the fruit. For crumbles, use your fingers for large clusters. For crisps, lightly press to adhere crumbs over the entire surface. Bake at 375°F for 35 to 45 minutes until the topping is deeply golden and the fruit juices bubble steadily. Allow at least 5 minutes of cooling – the topping will crisp further as steam escapes. Scoop warm crisp or crumble into bowls and top with ice cream, whipped cream, yogurt or zabaglione custard sauce. Of course, crisps and crumbles also work with savory fillings! Try roasted vegetables like cauliflower, carrots, parsnips, and Brussels sprouts pureed into a chunky mixture.

Well-seasoned potato and root vegetable latkes make hearty patties for a protein-rich bed topped with cheddar-Gruyere crisps. Sauteed greens, saucy chickpeas, or spiced lentils and beans covered with herby, cheesy or seed-packed crumbs are all delicious options. Cobblers take crisps up a notch by adding a tender biscuit topping over sweet, bubbling fruit. They are simple, rustic crowd-pleasers. You want a sturdy but flaky biscuit topping to soak up the fruit juices while retaining textural contrast. As we know, gluten development contributes to that tender-flaky balance, so gluten-free cobbler biscuits benefit from some special treatment. Adding one egg white to your biscuit dough gives structure through added protein without extra moisture – vital for biscuit texture. Tangzhong is an Asian technique using a cooked flour-and-water roux. Adding just a couple tablespoons of the thick paste also improves moisture distribution and structure in gluten-free baked goods like these biscuits. Start with 1-1/2 tablespoons of each flour and water gently cooked into a pliable putty. Cool before incorporating it into other dough ingredients. Lastly, keeping the biscuit dough quite cold before dropping and a hot oven for baking minimizes spreading for better rise and layering.

For the fruit filling, cobblers work best with juicy stone fruit and berries that will create plenty of sauce. Peaches and nectarines, apricots, plums and pluots, blackberries, blueberries, raspberries or a combination roasted for 10 to 15 minutes makes a fine foundation. Sweeten lightly with no more than ¼ cup sugar per 6 to 8 cups fruit. To assemble, pour the hot fruit and accumulated juices into a buttered 8 to 9-inch baking dish or iron skillet. Scoop out rough 2-tablespoon size dollops of the chilled biscuit dough and arrange evenly over the fruit.

Pour 2 tablespoons heavy cream around the edge and sprinkle the entire cobbler with a little sugar for glistening golden biscuits. Bake at 425 F, loosely covered with foil, for the first 15 to 20 minutes until biscuits have risen and firmed slightly, then remove the foil and continue baking 15 to 20 more minutes until deep golden brown. Individual bowls and ice cream servings are strongly recommended! And as with crisps and crumbles, cobbler toppings bring appeal over savory fillings too. Picture hearty beef and vegetable stews capped with cheddar biscuits. Spicy black bean and roasted vegetable chili topped with tender corn muffins. Or chunks of chicken, tomatoes, and greens baked under fluffy biscuit rounds for a satisfying meal. Buckles are a homey, old-fashioned single-layer fruit cake with a streusel-like cinnamon topping that "buckles" as it bakes. Yellow buckles traditionally showcase tart apples and pears, while darker fruit like blackberries, raspberries, and prunes lend their hues to brown or black buckles. Compared to multi-component crisps and cobblers, buckles offer simpler comfort with versatile gluten-free appeal. Good flavor and moist texture depend less on gluten development and more on high fruit content, beaten eggs for rise and structure and preventing tunneling from an overly thick batter. Sweet or tart orchard fruits, berries, and stone fruit all mix nicely into basic buckle batters. For the batter, base flour on lighter options like white rice flour, sorghum flour or superfine brown rice flour. Potato starch helps minimize gumminess that can develop from rice flour. And ground almonds or almond flour enrich the flavor and provide good protein balance to aid the lift from beaten eggs. Applesauce or mashed banana may replace some of the milk or yogurt for even greater moisture. Add spices like cinnamon, nutmeg, allspice, and ginger for warmth in darker buckles. Light brown or coconut sugar and molasses also boost flavor in a healthier fashion than granulated white sugar. Gently fold in fresh or thawed frozen fruits right at the end to preserve texture. Overmixing causes gluten-free batters to toughen.

To finish a buckle, sprinkle your favorite crumbly, crispy topping before baking. Try quick oats, brown sugar and cinnamon crumbs. Pulse nuts, coconut flakes, toffee bits, dried fruit, and brown sugar in the food processor for endless topping variations. Drizzle the finished buckle with a simple glaze of confectioner's sugar whisked with lemon juice and top with whipped cream or ice cream. Enjoy a warm buckle for breakfast or dessert any time of year!

Baking Fruit Cobblers and Buckles

When it comes to fruit cobblers, the biscuit topping steals much fanfare. But the luscious fruit filling deserves attention in its own right. Tailor the fruit prep to the variety at hand. Berries can be tossed raw right into a buttered baking dish. Their thin skins and abundance of juice take little help in becoming tender while retaining vivid flavor. Stone fruits like peaches, nectarines, plums and apricots benefit from 10 to 20 minutes of roasting in the oven first. Heat concentrates sugars and complex flavors while softening the flesh. Apples and pears need moisture to break down cellular structure after slicing. Toss cut fruit with a splash of water, cider, juice or wine, plus spices like cinnamon and nutmeg. After 20-30 minutes, the fruit will exude its own syrupy sauce, concentrating the liquid as it bakes further under the biscuit topping. And don't overlook savory cobbler fillings! For a crowd-pleasing pot pie cobbler hybrid, saute chicken, carrots, peas and pearl onions in a creamy sauce flavored with thyme and sherry. Ladle into a baking dish and top with your favorite gluten free biscuit variation before baking. Hearty vegetarian stews brimming with beans, lentils, squash, and greens make cheesy-herby biscuit toppers sing. Even mac and cheese gets an upgrade buried under craggy cheddar drop biscuits. Just be sure to drain excess liquid from savory fillings before topping and baking to prevent a soggy underside.

Fruit buckles may seem like simple, old-fashioned fare. But their charm and craveability make a case for keeping tradition alive. While any stone fruit or berries make fine fillings, apple buckles remain my personal preference. Choose firm, tart apples like Granny Smith, Pink Lady, or Honeycrisp to contrast the sweet spiced cake batter. Peel and dice into ½ to 1-inch chunks to create morsels of fruit throughout. Yellow and spiced brown sugar buckles typically call for cinnamon, but I recommend adding ginger, nutmeg and cloves as well. Their warmth draws out flavors of fall harvest apples gorgeously. A sprinkle of demerara sugar atop the buckle adds a glistening crunch with molasses notes to balance the sweetness. And serving warm apple buckle with tangy creme fraiche sets off the spice and brown sugar tones perfectly.

Berries – especially raspberries and blackberries - make excellent fillings, too with little prep needed. Gently crush about half the berries to release vivid juices that marble the cake with color and prevent a dry crumb. Leave the remaining berries whole for textural contrast. Lemon zest or a splash of juice balances their natural sweet-tartness. A touch of almond extract also pairs nicely with summer berries. Dollops of whipped cream or yogurt lend a nice tang as well.

Another way to incorporate produce into buckles is sweet vegetable purees. Cooked, mashed pumpkin, winter squash and sweet potatoes make wonderfully moist, flavorful additions to spice cakes. Carrots and zucchini also blend seamlessly into batters with added nutrition. For even more vegetable goodness, sneak a cup of grated zucchini or carrots into traditional apple buckles! The mild flavors meld into the background while adding natural sweetness and moisture to balance the starch and sugar. Just be sure to account for the extra liquid released from grated produce by patting it dry with paper towels before mixing it into dry ingredients.

But fruit hardly holds a monopoly when it comes to buckle inspiration. Savory buckles offer the same humble, homey appeal, using pantry staples for bright flavors and nutrition. To make a savory buckle base, replace some of the sugar with aromatic honey or maple syrup. Pump up the herbs, spices, and umami components such as tomato paste or nutritional yeast. Savory inclusions like caramelized onions or mushrooms, roasted vegetables, wilted spinach, and other greens create hearty, sliceable veggie cakes perfect for brunch or dinner. You can top them simply with crumbled feta or goat cheese. Or amp up the decadence factor with crispy bacon crumbles, sunflower or pumpkin seeds. The creative possibilities for sweet and savory gluten-free buckles are endless!

My friends, we've explored quite a range of humble, comforting fruit crisps, cobblers, and buckles without gluten! I hope these berry and apple visions danced through your mind's eye as we discussed proper fruit prep, tender-crisp toppings, and toothsome cake textures. Please try your hand at a classic peach cobbler, Homey Apple buckle, or modern veggie crisp this week. The pleasure of serving warm, bubbly fruit desserts in the age-old tradition of resourceful home bakers awaits your enjoyment! We'll shift gears next to the smooth, refined, and equally comforting realm of gluten-free puddings and custards in "Puddings, Mousses and Custards: Creamy and Comforting. That said, happy gluten-free baking to all!

Chapter 15

Puddings, Mousses, and Custards: Creamy and Comforting

With their sumptuously smooth texture and pure, uncomplicated sweetness, puddings and mousses represent the ultimate comforting treats. There's something nostalgic about them—they convey warmth, homeyness and ease. Yet despite their seemingly simple essence, creating well-crafted gluten-free puddings and mousses takes knowledge, care and the right touch.

In this chapter, we will unlock the secrets of making puddings with the ideal creamy-yet-firm texture and mousses that are light-as-air and melt in your mouth. We'll explore an array of flavor variations from chocolate to coconut and recipes both hot and chilled. You'll also learn tricks for preventing common issues like weepiness, cracking, curdling and deflation along the way.

Indulgent and Creamy Puddings and Mousses

While puddings and mousses appear similar—smooth, spoon able desserts—they differ fundamentally in technique and composition. Wonderfully rich, viscous pudding achieves its consistency and body through starch gelatinization. Gentle heating enables starch granules from gluten-free flours or starches like cornstarch, arrowroot or tapioca to swell and burst. As they release amylose and amylopectin, these long starch molecules tangle together throughout the surrounding liquid to form a network, thickening the mixture exponentially. The more swollen starch, the more viscosity and that satiny, creamy texture puddings are prized for.

By contrast, what gives ethereal mousse its melting delicate foaminess is the incorporation of air through whisking or folding. With ingredients like lightly whipped cream or beaten egg whites added, the resulting dessert remains feather-light yet stable. Eggs also lend added structure, as heat from a warm base like chocolate can denature proteins to unfurl and link up, also trapping air pockets. The interplay of starch, foam and coagulated egg proteins prevents the air bubbles from fully collapsing and water from separating for sliceable, quivering mousse.

Now, we'll explore techniques for flawless puddings and mousses in turn, from mixing methods to choice ingredients and preventative measures. Follow these methods and your puddings will shine satiny and smooth without clumping or weeping liquid. Your mousses will stand marvelously airy and substantially sliceable without deflating into soup. Read on for sweet, comforting creaminess made easy! Creamy and Comforting":

Baking Light and Tender Custards

Custards hold a special place in the pantheon of creamy desserts. Typically made with dairy and eggs gently heated to achieve thick, lush consistency, their pure, sweet flavor shines forth. Though often baked, custards can also be steamed or chilled after cooking over a water bath or double boiler. The resulting treat emerges satiny smooth, delicately set, and sublime.

Yet despite their seeming simplicity, custards require care to prevent curdling or overcooking into rubbery lumps. As the egg-enriched base heats, proteins start to coagulate while the remaining moisture steams, potentially leading proteins to bond too tightly and squeeze out liquid. Balancing time and temperature prevents this weeping. Gentle heating enables proteins to unfurl gradually so they encapsulate moisture, leaving the interior lusciously supple.

The most foolproof path to perfect baked custards lies in bathing. Setting ramekins or dishes in a hot water bath insulates delicately thickening custards from harsh oven air. Moist indirect heat lets them set slowly for an even texture without cracks or leaks. Nestle containers in a larger, rimmed pan and pour warm water about halfway up the sides. This moderates and distributes warmth so bases gently firm before barely set centers to finish setting. For smooth texture throughout, let custards wobble slightly when shaken rather than baking to total stiffness.

Choosing the right vessel also prevents overbaking. Thick, heavy ramekins conduct heat more slowly for gradual setting from the exterior in. Glass and ceramic work well too. Grease insides generously so custards slide out easily once cooled. If cracking appears during baking, tent foil overtop; residual heat will finish cooking centers without deepening flaws. Cooling too quickly risks cracks too, so let custards stand before chilling.

Ingredients influence texture immensely. As main components, egg yolks provide thickening proteins and fat for richness, while dairy lends moisture. Combining whole eggs and extra yolks makes for denser yet creamier results. Consider custard's final use too in choosing milk, cream or a blend. Heavy cream alone may overwhelm in elegant desserts but provides luscious base notes for pastry filling. Lastly, starches like cornstarch or tapioca prevent curdling by helping hold water in suspension.

When mixing, it helps to warm the dairy first for efficient blending. Slowly whisking hot liquid into yolks tempers them gradually. Once incorporated without scrambling, pouring the mixture back into the pot enables even heating to crucial coagulating temperatures. Just remember to stir frequently with a wooden spoon or heatproof spatula so protein strands can unfurl. Constant gentle motion prevents scorching as well as excess skin from forming on the surface.

For those short on time, instant defenses exist against curdling. While baking soda leaves a soapy aftertaste, lemon juice or cream of tartar brightens flavor while increasing acidity. The initial drop in pH causes proteins to unwind faster, so custards thicken cohesively before excessive heat causes them to recoil and separate. These preventative measures perfectly complement key strategies like water baths, greased containers and tempered mixing for dependably decadent results.

Whether featuring top notes of cinnamon, lemon verbena or Madagascar vanilla, custards manage to taste at once nostalgic yet innovative in their purity. Master proper preparations like gentle cooking so you can riff infinitely on this sweet, subtly infused creaminess canvas. Up next, we'll explore cheesecakes in all their ethereal lightness, followed by tips for layering and serving any creamy portion. So, let's unlock coveted recipes for all varieties of perfect cheesecakes and their fillings.

Chapter 16

Cheesecakes: Creamy, Smooth, and Satisfying

Baking the perfect gluten-free cheesecake requires finesse. With a tender, crumbly crust and lush, velvety filling, cheesecake seems decadent yet surprisingly light. Preparing one without gluten poses some unique challenges but also opens up creative possibilities with alternative flours and flavors. This chapter explores recipes, techniques, and tips for gluten-free cheesecake success.

Making the Perfect Gluten-Free Cheesecake Crust

Ah, the crust—that crisp, buttery foundation atop which a majestic cheesecake is constructed. More like a cookie than pastry, this component sets expectations for what's to come: flaky tenderness enrobing a rich, creamy interior.

Gluten-free crusts require thoughtful formulation as alternative flours lack proteins that enable elasticity and binding. Strategic mixing of various grains lends desirable texture and taste. The granularity of meals and starches must be balanced to avoid a crumble-prone or gummy base. As science and art collide in pastry, experimentation and observation are key.

Potential grain options include rice flour, sorghum flour, millet flour, teff flour, buckwheat flour, almond flour, coconut flour, and oat flour. Binding agents like xanthan gum or guar gum help adhesion. And flavor mediums like coconut oil or palm shortening enrich while substituting for gluten's elastic qualities. Sweeteners range from cane sugar to maple syrup to fruit purees.

Proportions of wet to dry will vary by recipe. However, efficient gluten development in wheat doughs must be substituted with delicate incorporation. Overworking can activate starches, causing a paste-like batter. Gentle blending to a coarse meal consistency allows oils to evenly coat.

Before filling and baking, prebaked crusts grant more stability. Blind baking solidifies structure and prevents a soggy bottom. Once cool, rims get coated in foil to thwart over-browning from extended oven time.

Crumble-prone textures come from excess moisture and heat. Reducing water content helps minimize this. Freezing doughs prior to press-forming boosts flakes, too. Covering crust edges when filling curtails saturation while protecting from curdling custards.

So, while crust necessitates some adjustments sans gluten, components can interplay beautifully, given proper ratios and technique. When done well, the tender crunch admirably introduces its luscious crown.

Baking Creamy and Smooth Cheesecake Fillings

When it comes to cheesecake texture, the filling defines distinction. Silkiness signifies success. So, discovering dairy-free alternatives to cream cheese brings its challenges. Most recipes spotlight ricotta, goat, quark, or vegan cream cheeses as bases. Each imparts unique qualities based on protein content, moisture, and fat. However, following proper mixing methods proves paramount for that desired creamy decadence. Blending the batter encourages smoothness and structure. Hand or stand variants work fine as long textures get integrated. Soft combining prevents overworking the proteins, though. Curdling or clumps come from aggressive agitation. Low and slow stirs minimize air pockets too. The order of wet and dry additions factors as well. Starting with the cheese allows the coating of remaining particulates. A third of the sugar joins next to avoid shocking milk proteins. Then, the eggs temper the mixture, lending emulsification. Alternating dry and wet layers afterward prevents lumps. Vanilla and citrus zest infuse when applicable. Proper incorporation means the custard coats a spoon, slowly drips, and leaves a visible trail. Too thick, and it clings heavily; too thin, it pours swiftly like cream. Finding the balance may require practice as moisture content fluctuates. But when done well, a pourable, lump-free batter emerges, ready for pan transfer.

Pre-baking cheesecake batters in either springform or tart pans allow customization. This bakes the exterior perimeter, forming clean slices without compromised structural integrity when served. Cracks come from rapid temperature changes, causing the interior to shrink faster than the solidifying crust. Low oven starts followed by increased heat minimize this. Water baths further moderate variance, insulating for gentler bakes. Covering with foil deters browning for softer curds, too. Inner rare cheesecakes stay decadently fudgy. Well-done styles take on a denser, drier consistency with more pronounced eggy notes. Personal preference guides doneness from nearly liquid centers to firmer styles. Checking centers at multiple timestamps grants better control. Mini cheesecakes satisfy both preferences simultaneously! And no matter the intent, cooling completely firms creamy fills before slicing or storage.

Infusing cheesecake batters generates interest through spices, herbs, vegetables, chocolate, caramel, or fruit purees. Consider the profile, though. Delicate berries pair better than assertive citruses, which may curdle dairy. Chunky swirls or layered designs incorporate nicely as well. Just save textural add-ins for last to retain structural security. Likewise, toppings lend additional flair. Sweet glazes, zesty coulis, nutty crumbles, or tart fruit compotes complete the elegant composition. For simple finishes, a dusting of cocoa or powdered sugar suffices.

In the end, gluten-free cheesecakes beg balance. Moving too fast risks bounds, while patience promises velvetiness. Once mastered, these cloud-like creations disappear quickly! Interpretations abound, but silkiness signifies success.

Chapter 17

Ice Creams and Sorbets: Chilly Treats

On a hot summer day, few treats are as refreshing as a heaping scoop of creamy, rich ice cream or a tart and fruity sorbet. These frozen desserts cool you down in an instant and satisfy your sweet tooth with their sweet, creamy, or fruity profiles.

While traditional ice creams rely on ingredients like dairy, eggs, and sugar that can be challenging for those eating gluten-free, have no fear - with a few clever substitutions and techniques, you can craft ice creams and sorbets that will rival any you've tried before. This chapter takes the chill off of gluten-free frozen desserts, exploring how to concoct crave-worthy scoops at home.

Part 1: Making Ice Creams

Close your eyes and imagine slowly licking an ice cream cone as beads of sweat drip down its sides on a hot and humid day. The sweet, icy cream coats your tongue in lush vanilla, rich chocolate or sweet strawberry as you instantly feel refreshed. Now open your eyes and grab a mixing bowl and spatula because I'll walk you through crafting creamy, rich ice creams without gluten or dairy that will satisfy any frozen craving. We'll start with the basics of ice cream construction - the all-important base.

Traditional ice cream bases contain egg yolks, dairy milk or cream, and sugar. As many gluten and dairy-free folks know, replicating the fat and protein content to achieve that signature creamy richness can be tricky without those ingredients. But with clever substitutions like coconut milk, nut milk, bananas, and avocados, we can mirror the texture and decadence. The keys are nailing the right ratio of fat to liquid for your chosen base along with incorporating stabilizing agents like guar or xanthan gum to prevent icy crystals.

I'll offer a classic custard-style base along with a thicker avocado-based blend. Pick the one that aligns best with your dietary needs, and each churns up satisfyingly creamy. A Guide to Delectable Gluten-Free Treats":

Part 2: Creating Refreshing Sorbets

Just as ice cream offers a creamy reprieve from summer's heat, sorbets present the perfect cool, fruity balance with their bright, sweet-tart flavors and smooth texture free of fat or cream. Ranging from bold berries to tropical fruits like mango, sorbets highlight nature's bounty at their best. As sugar and fruit form their base, they couldn't be simpler to craft at home. Once you master a couple of straightforward techniques, you can churn up endless flavor variations.

We'll begin with fruit selection, which serves as the foundation of sensational sorbets. Seek out ripe, seasonal picks bursting with vivid colors and aromas at farmers' markets, if possible, for superior flavor. Tree fruits like peaches, plums, and apricots transition beautifully, while citrus like oranges, grapefruit and lemons ensure plenty of tangy juice.

Berries never disappoint - try swapping strawberries for raspberries or combining cherries with blackberries. Tropical choices like mangoes, pineapple, and kiwi also shine frozen in a sorbet. Just avoid melons, which tend to get icy rather than smooth and creamy when churned.

Prep your fruit by washing, hulling, seeding, and chopping it into small pieces before pureeing until smooth. Citrus sorbets utilize fresh squeezed juice - making them great for imperfect fruits with plenty of juice inside. Simmer chopped fruit with a bit of water for 10 minutes until softened, then puree it. Straining removes excess solids and seeds - I prefer some tiny flecks but a super smooth texture works too.

With fruit puree in hand, adding a sweetener is next. Granulated sugar dissolves easily, but brown sugar, honey, or maple syrup contribute lovely caramel notes. Corn syrup helps prevent iciness, but I suggest using just a small amount. Start with ¾ to 1 cup of sweetener per 4 cups of fruit puree, then tweak it to your preferred level of sweetness. Infusing the milk with aromatic spices like cinnamon, vanilla, or cardamom enhances the sorbet beautifully.

Stir your sweetened puree, then chill it thoroughly for at least 4 hours. Quick chilling in an ice bath accelerates the process if you're impatient. Once completely cooled, freeze your base according to your ice cream maker's instructions for about 20-30 minutes. This aerates the sorbet as tiny ice crystals form while maintaining a scoopable texture. Et voila, refreshing, fruit-packed sorbets are ready to enjoy! Though sorbet lacks dairy, adding a touch of lemon juice mimics buttermilk's tangy flavor, while a spoonful of nut butter contributes creaminess. Go ahead and experiment with mix-ins like chocolate chunks, crumbled cookies, or herbs, too if you'd like.

Endless flavor options await your imagination - I suggest keeping a few containers of sorbet base on hand. Try swapping berries for stonefruits or citrus one week and tropical fruits the next for a delicious variety all season long! With such simple ingredients and methods, a batch of vibrant, not-too-sweet sorbet offers a cool reprieve from summer's swelter time.

Chapter 18

Pastry: Savory and Sweet

As we dive deeper into the wide world of gluten-free pastry, an essential place to begin is understanding the foundation - the dough itself. Gluten-free pastry dough can seem intimidating at first. Without gluten to provide structure, achieving that coveted flakiness takes some finesse. But once you grasp a few key techniques for both sweet and savory versions, you'll find yourself whipping up crusts fit for a king's court.

Our journey starts with the holy trinity of ingredients used in nearly all pastry recipes - flour, fat, and liquid. While the options seem simple enough, their ratios and combinations make all the difference. Gluten-free flours lack strength, so binding agents replace some of the flour to add elasticity. Meanwhile, solid fats like butter or shortening create those delicate, flaky layers by coating dough strands during mixing and baking. Finally, liquid ingredients such as water, milk or eggs hydrate the dough while allowing the solid fats to seamlessly integrate.

When combined properly, these basic components meld into a supple and moldable gluten-free dough perfect for lining pie pans or encasing fillings. As we explore recipes, pay attention to the texture and feel of each dough. With practice, you'll learn to adjust moisture, fat, or binders to achieve your ideal consistency. Now, let's get mixing!

Sweet Pastry 101

Sweet pastries make dream desserts - think fruit and custard pies, elegant tarts with velvety fillings, crispy palmiers, and more. Their subtly sweet dough provides the perfect complement to bold flavors and textures. To craft stellar gluten-free versions, follow a few fundamental rules.

First, choose your flours. A blend of white rice flour, tapioca starch and potato starch gives both structure and tenderness. The rice flour offers graininess to mimic wheat flour, while the starches contribute binding power and lightness. Some recipes also incorporate almond flour or cornstarch for extra stability. Just ensure your blend isn't overly starchy or heavy.

Next, cut the butter into the flour. Whether using your fingertips, a blender or a food processor, you want pea-sized pieces thoroughly coated. Larger bits melt during baking, creating those coveted air pockets. Aim for visible chunks rather than a fine meal, which would toughen the crust.

Finally, avoid overworking the dough. Once liquid is added, handle gingerly to keep those butter layers intact. Press into the desired shape without kneading, then chill thoroughly before baking. This helps firms the dough for easy transferring.

Follow these guidelines, and your gluten-free crusts will rival their glutenous counterparts. Still, seem intimidating? Start with a simple tart crust or palmiers to build confidence. We'll tackle more complex constructions soon enough!

Savory Pastry Pointers

While their dessert cousins may get more glory, savory pastries like pot pies, quiches, and handheld appetizers certainly deserve attention. Thankfully, most techniques still apply with a few tweaks.

Nutrient-dense flours like sorghum, millet, or amaranth make excellent bases for hearty crusts. Buckwheat and teff also supply earthiness for savory dishes. Just ensure your blend includes a binding agent like xanthan gum or psyllium husk to prevent crumbling.

Additionally, swap out some butter for shortening or lard. Their neutral flavors keep crusts meltingly tender without competing with bold ingredients. Mix in grated cheese or spices for extra dimension.

Chilling the dough remains vital to maintain structure once filled, so refrigerate thoroughly. Carefully score vent holes before baking to allow steam to escape from juicy contents.

Follow these savory suggestions, and your gluten-free pot pies will have everyone begging for seconds. Flaky, buttery rounds of spanakopita or mushroom galettes also showcase gluten-free dough's versatility.

Rolling and Shaping Techniques

With stellar dough comes the fun part - rolling, filling and decoratively crimping your gluten-free creations. While special pans or rings help form perfect rounds, don't be afraid to hand-shape free-form galettes. Rustic edges charm guests while saving hassle.

If using pie pans, first grease then line with parchment paper or foil before adding dough. Press into edges, trim excess then decoratively crimp sides by pinching with fingers or using a fork. Add weights like rice or beads when pre-baking.

For galettes, shape dough into rounds on parchment, then top with desired fillings, leaving a 2-inch border. Fold edges up and over, pleating as you rotate. Brush with egg wash and sprinkle sugar or spices.

Other impressive tricks include braiding strips for lattice-topped treats or intricately shaping twists, palmiers, and pinwheels using a well-chilled dough. Use cookie cutters on rolled sheets to make shaped appetizer bites.

To serve, drizzle specialty glazes or dust with powdered sugar for added panache.

Troubleshooting Tricky Doughs

Of course, with all these shaping methods come potential pitfalls. But have no fear! Here is your guide to diagnosing and fixing the most common issues when working with gluten-free dough:

Crumbling dough - Too little liquid or binding agent
* Slowly work in drops of ice water and let rest 5 minutes to hydrate
* Sprinkle on additional xanthan gum if needed

Tough, rubbery dough - Overmixed
* Avoid kneading once liquid is added
* Refrigerate to relax gluten, then gently re-roll

Won't roll out easily - Too stiff

* Allow sitting at room temperature 10-15 minutes to soften
* Carefully knead in drops of water if still too firm

Shrinking in pan - Warm dough
* Chill thoroughly before transferring and baking
* If pre-baked, add parchment and pie weights

Soggy bottom crust - Too much moisture
* Use cornstarch or tapioca starch to absorb excess
* Bake on preheated sheet or pizza stone

With these handy tips, your gluten-free dough frustrations will dissolve. Now, let's finally bite into some flakey gluten-free deliciousness!

Savory Starters

Few summer sensations satisfy, like biting into a crispy spanakopita triangle with its spinach and feta filling barely contained by countless flaky layers. Or waking up to a cast iron skillet of quiche oozing with melty Gruyere and bacon, perfuming your whole kitchen.

While typically wheat-based, these iconic appetizers beautifully crossover to the gluten-free side when made with a few easy substitutions.

Sweet Sensations

Now for the best part - dessert! Visions of berry pies, towering croquembouche, and palmiers likely danced through your mind. Well, with some gluten-free dough demystified, let's start baking!

Savory and sweet pastries alike showcase gluten-free baking's endless potential for flakiness. As you experiment with doughs, embrace creativity and have fun forming sizes from petite to colossal! Soon, these techniques will feel like second nature, leaving you ready to tackle any shape or recipe you desire.

Chapter 19

Breads Around the World: Global Gluten-Free

When it comes to bread, the tradition has a lengthy history rooted in antiquity. From the cultivation of grains to baking them in every imaginable form, breads represent the universal symbols of nourishment, sustenance, and sustaining life. So, what about gluten-free breads and their role throughout history? As the need for wheat-free options emerged, local resources and regional creativity led to countless variations on bread themes across civilizations and cultures worldwide. While gluten intolerance is a relatively new concept, ancient baking practices focused on available local grain goods, which happened to often lack gluten. Traditionally rice flour, buckwheat flour, millet flour, almond flour, chickpea flour, nut flour, and more were commonly incorporated in creating breads for village consumption.

This ancient reliance on basics is fundamentally responsible for a global diversity of naturally gluten-free breads from the start. By visiting the historical relationship of longstanding bread traditions, we gain insight into accessible resources for crafting hearty loaves today, inspired by the bounty of ingredients surrounding early bakers. Along with honoring timeless techniques, the absence of gluten emerged less as a targeted end goal and more as a product of traditional regional elements.

As a result, gluten-free fare was widespread simply in its common exclusion of high-gluten wheat. Cultures across the Mediterranean rim, Southeast Asia, Scandinavia, India's Subcontinent, and more reflect this. Their reliance on basic grains and other food items ushered in innovative gluten-free creations organically and often out of necessity in the local surroundings. By exploring this robust global history, you gain an enriched awareness that you're in good company in crafting and enjoying gluten-free breads today.

Ancient Origins, Lasting Impact: Early Gluten-Free Breads & Grains

From Mesopotamia's first leavened breads to ancient Egypt and India, many early bread varieties lacked gluten out of reliance on simple, accessible goods rather than conscious health aims. Two naturally gluten-free options rose to prominence very early on:

The first, millet, dates back over 10,000 years, tracing origins to northern China, where Neolithic residents enjoyed it toasted, in porridge and baked in flat bread. Highly sustainable, it traveled west by Asian trade routes, reaching Europe by 3,000 BCE. Resistant, fast-growing, and hardy, its lack of gluten and digestive benefits made it a lifesaving staple across China, India, Africa, and more.

The second, rice, domesticated equally early in the Yellow River region, also quickly spread, becoming a defining crop of Chinese civilization by 2,800 BCE. Glutinous rice was favored for baking sturdy steamed breads and sweeter treats, while non-glutinous short-grain rice defined Eastern and Southeast Asian cuisines. Each variety was rich in nutrition, naturally gluten-free, and versatile for myriad applications, especially breads and noodles. With rice as their staple crop, they enjoyed naturally gluten-free diets by default through the ages.

Beyond foundational grains like millet and rice, numerous other gluten-free goods served as widespread ancient staples due to regional accessibility. From nourishing flours to binding agents, here's a tasting tour of global gluten-free mainstays through history and their lasting legacies tasted today.

Sorghum: Sub-Saharan Staple Turned Global Phenomenon

While millet reigned supreme across much of Asia and rice defined Eastern fare, sorghum emerged as a defining crop of Sub-Saharan Africa due to its resilience. This ancient cereal grain thrives where other crops struggle, surviving heat, drought, floods and more. Archaeological evidence traces its domestication back over 8,000 years to Northeast Africa's Nabta Playa region.

As Bantu farmers migrated south and east between 1000 BCE and 500 CE, they brought sorghum growing expertise turning the grain into a staple crop of these regions over two millennia. Compared to millet, sorghum offers higher protein levels and digestibility yet with similarly impressive vitamin and mineral content. When ground into flour, it also notably lacks gluten making it ideal for unleavened flatbreads, porridges, baked goods and thicker beers.

While sorghum only reached Europe and the U.S. in the mid 19th century, today it ranks as the world's fifth largest cereal grain crop. This ancient hardy cereal endures as a gluten-free and vegan baking essential, useful in everything from hearty seeded bread loaves to ginger molasses cookies. Its natural absence of gluten and high protein elevates it as especially valuable for gluten-free flour blends.

Teff Love: Tiny Seed, Big Impact from Ethiopia to Mainstream

While sorghum provisioned Sub-Saharan societies for ages, teff emerged in the Ethiopian Highlands by 4,000 BCE transforming regional cuisine. The world's smallest grain, each reddish-brown teff seed measures just over a millimeter wide harboring an outsized nutritional impact. Resilient to difficult growing conditions, it grew vital for the livelihood and cuisine of northern and central Ethiopia as well as Eritrea.

Teff not only withstands Ethiopia's challenges but actually thrives, growing well in both waterlogged and dry soils. Compared to wheat, teff boasts higher calcium, protein, and fiber levels and can be substituted for almost any grain product. Naturally gluten-free, teff grounded into flour proves fundamental for beloved Ethiopian gluten-free delicacies.

Injera, a sourdough spongy flatbread made solely from teff flour and water, serves as the cornerstone of Ethiopian dining. Its subtle tang and signature porous texture provide perfect utensil-free scooping of spicy wots (stews) and flavorful noshes. Beyond injera, teff stars in everything from yogurt flatbreads to stews and whole grain porridges.

While teff remained an Ethiopian secret for centuries, growing in popularity only in neighboring countries, it started garnering global fame as Ethiopian restaurants spread worldwide. Today, as the West adopts traditionally gluten-free goods for new health aims, teff is now grown and enjoyed in India, Australia, South Africa, Idaho, and beyond!

Cassava: Caribbean and Latin American Gluten-Free Staple

Just as sorghum fed vast swaths of Africa and teff-filled platters in the Horn of Africa, cassava roots became a defining staple across Latin America and the Caribbean. Though central Brazil marks cassava's origins over 7,000 years ago, this woody shrub flourished not only in South America but across Southeast Asian and Caribbean climes, too.

Thanks to Portuguese traders who likely brought varieties from Brazil in the 16th century, cassava cultivation boomed in tropical locales from sub-Saharan Africa to Indonesia. This versatile tuber adapted wonderfully to poor soils, proving reliably productive even during droughts, ideal for impoverished regions historically. High levels of calcium, carbohydrates, and vitamin C endeared it, yet the most important aspect was its lack of gluten.

Grate the starchy white tubers, squeeze out the liquid and let it ferment, then form dough and bake it into staples across cultures. In the Caribbean, fine cassava flour proves perfect for gluten-free petit pain rolls and haitian patties' flaky dough plus Dominican casabe flatbreads. Meanwhile, in Brazil, tapioca flour from cassava creates chewy, gluten-free pão de queijo cheese breads and garlicky broa de fubá cornmeal bread.

Cassava even stars in Vietnamese Bánh khoai mì pancakes, Thai khao phat fried rice cakes and putu mayam noodle cakes popular in Malaysia and Indonesia. Today, cassava remains cherished for its hardy-growing nature, flexible uses in baking and cooking, and reliably gluten-free appeal.

Wild Rice: Native American Aquatic Grain Gift

Of course, no gluten-free bread tour proves complete without wild rice, a prized aquatic seed rich in lore. Technically an annual grass, not rice, North America's Upper Great Lakes region and Canada hosts aquatically growing wild rice for ages, with traces dating over 9,000 years. Hundreds of years ago, prophecies mandated Native Americans share this vitamin and protein-packed seed only with outsiders facing starvation.

Soon, the Ojibwa, Chippewa, Sioux, and Winnebago tribes came to rely heavily on its nutty flavor and hard yet fast-growing nature. Traditional harvesting continues today, with reservations boasting wild rice-focused cultures and cuisine. Beyond serving as a base for breads and cereals, wild rice stars are a hearty addition to fillings, too.

It joins turkey, cranberries, and walnuts in festive Thanksgiving stuffings across America. Meanwhile, Ojibwa agers down it as a base for seasonal venison or duck meat pies' fillings, often wrapped in a flaky pastry crust without gluten. Swedish and German immigrants baked it into Vensk limpa rye-less rye breads and earthy pumpernickel loaves in Minnesota, a land of sky-blue waters and wild rice galore.

Thanks to its aquatic origins and strong regional ties, wild rice brings a distinct hearty flavor, chewy texture, and stellar nutritional benefits to bread baking across cultures. Discover wild rice's wonders in multigrain sandwich loaves and nutty cornbread squares, or simply enjoy its nutritious heft by steaming spoonfuls in a rich stew or porridge anytime.

Cassava, sorghum, teff, wild rice, and more grains shine light on the diverse possibilities of gluten-free baking across lands and time. At the same time, once geography limited ingredients, today's global markets unlock the limitless potential to blend worldly flours and techniques into your very own kitchen. Taste the spongy tang of Ethiopian injera, chew sweet Brazilian cheese bread, or savor the earthy nuttiness of wild rice breads by simply perusing flour aisles with openness to adventure.

Ingredients are now within closer reach; what will you bake?

Chapter 20

Holiday Baking: Celebrations Without Gluten

The winter holidays often center around beloved baked goods, from fruited cakes to gingerbread cookies. When you start following a gluten-free diet, it can feel like you need to give up these special treats. However, with some creative substitutions and recipe tweaks, you can keep those tasty holiday traditions alive. This chapter will explore ways to make your favorite holiday bakes gluten-free, as well as discover exciting new recipes to add to your seasonal spread.

As you start your gluten-free holiday baking adventure, keep an open mind. While classic recipes like pumpkin pie or cranberry sauce likely just need minor adjustments to make them GF, other baked goods like breads, cookies, and some dense cakes may need more modifications. Don't be afraid to experiment and try out alternative flours like almond, coconut, or chickpea flour rather than sticking solely to rice or tapioca options. Playing with extracts, spices, zests, nuts, dried fruits, and more can also lend new flavors to your old standbys or holiday bakes.

Stock Up for Success

When it comes to gluten-free holiday baking, proper planning and smart ingredient choices are key. Before you preheat that oven, take stock of your kitchen tools and dry storage. Ensure you have the essential equipment's like parchment paper, cupcake liners, and nonstick pans, as GF flours tend to stick more. Restock any flours, leaveners, thickeners, and sweeteners you rely on for baking. Also, stock up on extracts, spices, zests, nuts, and dried fruits to flavor your holiday treats.

Here are some must-have ingredients for gluten-free holiday bakes:

All-purpose GF flour - Choose a trusted, cup-for-cup blend you enjoy baking with. Bob's Red Mill, King Arthur, Betty Crocker, and Glutino all offer quality mixes.

Xanthan and guar gums - Just 1/2 to 1 teaspoon of these magical powders can help give structure, moisture, and lift to GF baked goods. Don't skip them! Have some neutral oil like canola or vegetable as well as butter on hand for baking gluten-free treats. Some recipes work best with one or the other. Eggs help bind and leaven GF goodies, while milk, cream, yogurt, and sour cream add moisture, flavor, and lift.

Be sure to have your sweetener bases covered, too, from white and brown sugars to maple syrup and honey, which all lend nuances to gluten-free baked items.

Flavor boosters - Stock up on vanilla, almond, lemon, orange and other extracts. Toss in cinnamon, nutmeg, ginger, cardamom, and any baking spices you enjoy too. Dried fruits, nuts, coconut, and chocolate chips make a tasty mix-in too.

Rethink Holiday Favorites

Once you're armed with the right kitchen tools and ingredients, it's time to start playing with recipes. Rather than trying to perfectly recreate Grandma's plum pudding, embrace this as an opportunity to develop new traditions. Breathe fresh life into old classics with creative substitutes. Or better yet, discover and fall in love with new gluten-free holiday recipes.

When revisiting old family favorites, keep an open mind to rethinking every element - even seemingly GF ingredients like fruits or dairy. Cross-contamination is common. Consider making your own cranberry sauce from scratch rather than using canned options with questionable assembly lines. Choose fresh fruits versus mystery-ingredient baked pies. Love Aunt Edna's ambrosia salad? Recreate it using your trusted GF sugar cookies instead of store-bought varieties that may contain hidden gluten.

Some holiday classics will come together more easily than others when made gluten-free. Dishes that are naturally GF, like roast turkey and gravy, mashed potatoes, roasted autumn vegetables, salads, and many soups just need minor tweaks. Avoid adding wheat-flour thickened roux to gravies or breadcrumb toppings to casseroles. Check broth ingredients for surprise wheat, too.

Meanwhile, others like bread stuffing, warm fruit puddings, wheat flour biscuits, and rolls will require more substitutions. Use cornbread, GF bread cubes, or rice as your base for stuffing instead. Swap wheat biscuits for fluffy GF versions made with your favorite blend. Choose naturally GF desserts like custards, meringue pies, custard, and ice cream-based treats over fussy fruitcakes. Or better yet, dive into our GF yeasted bread options in Chapter 5. With the right techniques, you can have beautiful gluten-free rolls or baguettes for holiday meals.

Explore New Traditions

While navigating old favorites, also consider adding new gluten free dishes to your holiday rotation. Rethink tired appetizers like cheese balls or wheat cracker spreads. Whip up fresh GF crackers with rosemary and sea salt or cheese, and herbed popcorn for nibbling. Make a show-stopping veggie platter with a hummus dip. Stuff mushrooms, peppers or mini potatoes for a cute, gluten-free finger-food option even kids devour.

Salads and sides can also steal the gluten-free show. Brighten up meals with roasted beets over crisp greens with tangy goat cheese. Bake sweet potatoes with pecans, maple syrup, and cranberries for a festive fall twist. Remember, most simple veggies, grains like rice or quinoa and salad mixes make ideal starting points for naturally gluten-free sides. Just avoid heavily processed versions with unwanted additives.

Dearest baker, we've come a long way, and your success is not so far away. All you need to do right now is to sit up and take the first step. In no time, you'll be making headway in the world of baked recipes. I wish you massive success!